THE MERCANTILE PALACE
OF
H. G. MUNGER & CO.
A HISTORY OF THE MUNGER'S DEPARTMENT STORE
142 North Main Street, Herkimer, NY
1869 - 1970
AND BEYOND
Researched & Written by
Thomas Lee Johnson

ACKNOWLEDGEMENTS

I would like to acknowledge the following for their support and help in bringing the history of Herkimer's **H. G. Munger & Co**. department store to life:

Joseph Chilelli, current owner of the **Munger's** building; **Christine Fleischer, Frank J. Basloe Library Director, Herkimer, NY,** and staff members **Deb West, Rebekah M.** and staff; **Herkimer County Historical Society: Cassandra Castle, Executive Director; Kathy Huxtable,** a **volunteer**; and the entire staff.

Melanie Lopata, owner/operator of Get It Write Publishing Company for turning this book into reality.

Also, **James S. Pitcher, Boonville, NY, Town Historian; Shari Peto** of the **Gloversville Public Library, Gloversville, NY; Mary Ann Terzi** and the staff of the **Little Falls Historical Society**, Little Falls, NY; and **Gary King**, whose family once owned the **Munger's** building.

I would especially like to acknowledge my wife, **Mary**, for helping me with proofreading.

GUIDE

In writing this book, I have **acknowledged all sources** when known. Any omissions, errors and/or **copyright infringements are unintentional**.

All text within each chapter, in **italics**, is a **direct quote** from the given source. Some misspelled words, colloquialisms, or rural slang within the italicized quote are left as written in the original, but an attempt was made to correct obvious typos and grammar.

When a "**direct quote**" is prefixed with the wording "**in part,**" it means that not all the content of that source pertaining to a given subject is included. Parts may be left out due to their redundancy, or in the cases pertaining to old newspapers, because certain parts are unreadable due to the poor quality of the original when scanned onto microfiche.

TABLE OF CONTENTS

INTRODUCTION

Although **Henry Gillette Munger** didn't originate the concept of the **department store**, when he opened his first store back in **1869**, it was still a new-fangled idea that many people in smaller communities had never witnessed.

In short order, **H. G. Munger & Co.'s New York store** became one of the largest such establishments in **Herkimer County** and beyond.

Munger's was not just a department store, but for many, it was an experience that took them from their everyday humdrum existence into a fabulous shopping experience likened to entering a grand palace.

Over the many years of H. G. Munger & Co.'s store's existence, hundreds, if not thousands, of satisfied customers looked forward to such an outing.

In a newspaper account of the opening of Munger's newly refurbished store in conjunction with their **70th anniversary** celebration in **1939**, the store itself was described as a "**Mercantile Palace.**"

An earlier newspaper article in **1887** described **H. G. Munger** as "**The Merchant Prince of Herkimer County.**"

Henry Gillette Munger was indeed the **Merchant Prince of Herkimer County** for many years, holding court in his **Mercantile Palace** on North Main Street in downtown Herkimer, NY.

Today, the building that once housed **Munger's Department Store** is still fondly remembered as "**Munger's**" by the citizens of Herkimer, NY, many of whom are too young to have ever remembered a time when the store was in operation.

Helping to keep the **Munger's** name alive is present owner **Joseph Chilelli**, who for the past several years has worked tirelessly to bring back life to the old building, which he has accomplished, although much work still needs to be done.

This book stands as a testament to Chilelli's hard work and to the legacy of **H. G. Munger & Co.'s** department store.

On the following pages is the story of **Henry Gillette Munger**, "**The Merchant Prince of Herkimer County**," and his "**Mercantile Palace.**"

Enjoy,
Thomas Lee Johnson

H. G. Munger
Pictured center with right hand to waist.
[Date and Herkimer Location Unknown]

The Different Locations

that the H. G. Munger & Co. occupied
on North Main Street, Herkimer, NY
From 1869 to Present

Map Researched, Drawn/Assembled by
Thomas L. Johnson
[Map Not Drawn to Scale]

[1]
First Location
Fox Block
[North of and next to the Waverly Hotel]
Hotel pictured far right
May 1869 – 1891

[2]
Second Location:
Herkimer National Bank Block
NE Corner of North Main & Green St.
1891 – Feb. 26, 1898

Green Street

Green Street

North Main Street

Mary Street

Mary Street

North Main Street

North Main Street

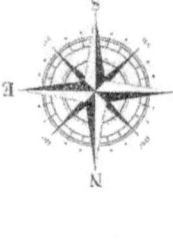

Frank J. Basloe Library
245 N. Main St.
[Used as a point of reference.]

Palmer House Hotel
269 N. Main St.
[Used as a point of reference.]

*Only the areas which pertain to identifying the location history of
the H. G. Munger & Co., along North Main St., in Herkimer, NY, are
shown on this map.

Map
Drawn & Assembled
October 2023

Map continuing south on North Main St. next page.....

The Different Locations

that the H. G. Munger & Co. occupied on North Main Street, Herkimer, NY

From 1869 to Present

Map Researched, Drawn/ Assembled by

Thomas L. Johnson

[Map Not Drawn to Scale]

[3]

L to R: The Earl Block (Moved into May 1899), Masonic Temple Block (Moved into May 1904) and Graves Block (Moved into March 1904), before the completion of the Masonic Temple.

In February 1917, a fire destroyed the Earl and Masonic Temple Block's and damaged the Graves Block, although Munger's Store in the Graves Block was still able to conduct business. In designing the new Munger's building, the Graves Block was incorporated into the blueprints and Judge Graves home was razed along with all buildings between the Graves and Grogan Block. Whether the extended one floor storefront, to the right of the Graves Block, housing the Munger's Shoe Store, was also incorporated into the new Graves design or razed along with the Judge Graves house, is not known.

North Main Street

Green Street

North Main Street

[4]

In 1918, the new Munger & Co. department store opened. In 1922, the Grogan Block, adjoining the new store on its right, was purchased. The two stores were then joined together on the second floor through an archway which had been constructed. The second floor of the Grogan Block was then used as a Furniture Department for Munger's. A dance school occupied the third floor and the old defunct opera house on the top or fourth floor in 1946, a third floor was added to the main Munger's building. In 1957, after the W. T. Grant store vacated the first floor of the opera house building, Munger's connected their building with the Grogan Block (Opera House Block) on the ground floor. Now the Furniture Department occupies the first two floors.

Park Avenue

S Main St.

W State Street

Albany Street

W. State Street

Albany Street

*Only the areas which pertain to identifying the location history of the H. G. Munger & Co., along North Main St., in Herkimer, NY, are shown on this map.

Map
Drawn & Assembled
October 2023

S

E

N

W

CHAPTER ONE
HENRY GILLETTE MUNGER'S FORMATIVE YEARS

[The Early Evolution of the H. G. Munger Department Store, Herkimer, NY]

A Short Family History Lesson

Henry Gillette Munger, future founder of one of the biggest department stores in the Mohawk Valley, was born on **March 28, 1846**, in the small village of **Camden, Oneida Co., NY.**

His father, **Jairus H. Munger**, a farmer who became a prominent attorney, was born on **October 7, 1812**, in **Fenner, Madison Co., NY**, a son of **Jothan** (1787-1862) and **Elizabeth** (maiden name unknown) **Munger** (1789-1839).

Jothan and **Elizabeth Munger** would have five known children: **Jairus H. Munger** (1812-1876), **Mary J. Munger** (1815-1842), **Arvilla Munger** (1817-1872), **Rufus Munger** (1819-1859) and **Linus Munger** (1822-1842).

Jairus H. Munger, a Republican, was a prominent lawyer, serving for many years as **Camden's District Attorney**, having first been elected in **1857**. He partnered in the law firm of **Munger & Becker**. Their office was located at **60 Main St., 2nd floor, Camden, NY.**, according to the **1869 Business Directory for Oneida Co., NY.**

Jairus would also establish a law practice in **Rome, Oneida Co., NY**.

Around **March** of **1864, Munger & Becker** began publishing **The Camden Journal**, a weekly newspaper that cost its readers $1 per annum in advance. **Jairus H. Munger** was the editor of the paper, a job that he held until his death. Following his death in **1876**, the paper continued publishing until **1884**.

Jairus H. Munger died on **October 28, 1876**, Camden, Oneida Co., NY. He is buried at the **Forest Park Cemetery** in Camden.

Henry Gillette Munger's mother, **Lilian Irene (nee Gillette) Munger,** was born on **April 4, 1820**, in **Fenner, Madison Co., NY.** She was the daughter of **Daniel M.** (1782-1853) and **Lydia Leach** (nee **Park**) **Munger** (1780-1866).

Jairus H. and **Lilian Irene Munger** would have five known children: **Henry G. Munger** (1846-1933), **Mary Elizabeth Munger** (1850-1940), **Clifford J. Munger** (1854-1856), **Charles Sumner**

Munger (1856-1929), and **Lilian (also known as Lily) Irene Munger** (1858-1860).

Lily Irene Munger, Jairus's wife, died on **February 7, 1899, Dunkirk, NY**. She is buried at the **Forest Park Cemetery** in Camden.

Henry's Schooling

Henry Gillette Munger grew up in the village of **Camden, Oneida Co., NY.**, attending public school(s) there.

He later completed his education at the **Falley Seminary**, a boarding school, in **Fulton, Oswego Co., NY.** The school was established in **1836** as the "**Fulton Female Seminary**," a girls' only preparatory school operated by the Presbyterian church. In **1842**, the school started accepting male students as well and was renamed the **Fulton Academy**. In **1849**, the **Methodist Church Conference** took over the school, naming it the **Falley Seminary** after **Mrs. M. E. Falley**, who gifted the school **$3,000** (equivalent today to **$97,716**).

H. G. Munger Traveling the Road to Success

At the young age of fourteen or fifteen (**1859/60**), Henry started his lifelong career in the mercantile business, clerking full-time in the employment of **Anson Gates (A.G.) Olmstead**, a dry goods merchant in **Camden, NY**. Here he would remain for the next year and a half.

A.G. Olmstead, born on **Feb. 11, 1815, Delhi, Delaware**, came to **Camden** in **1844**, from his home in **Sandy Creek, Oswego Co., NY,** with his wife, **Almira** (nee **Plumley** 1816-1851), and then two children: **Fayette Wayne Olmstead** (1840-1912) and **Maronette P. Olmstead** (1844-1927).

In Camden, Anson established himself in the dry goods trade.

Here, **Anson** and **Almira** would have two more children, daughters: **Mary Aurelia Olmstead** (1846-1905) and **Frances Olmstead** (1851-1942).

Following the death of his wife, Almira, in **1851**, Anson remarried. His second wife was **Martha F. Cropsey** (1831-1861). They had three known children: **William D. Olmstead** (1855-?), **Claudia Olmstead** (1858-?), and **George C. Olmstead** (1859-1916).

After **Martha** died in **1861**, Anson married **Melinda Lathers** (1836-1926) on **May 28, 1862**. There were no known children in this marriage.

At some point, Anson would partner with his son **Fayette** in the clothing business in Camden.

The **1860 Oneida County Business Directory** lists: *A. G. Olmstead, clothier and dealer in gents' furnishing goods, agent for sewing machines. 71 Main Street, Camden.*

Another source, **Daniel Elbridge Wagner's Our Country and Its People: A descriptive work on Oneida County, New York,** online lists a "**Olmstead & Meacham, Clothier**" in Camden.

Author's Notes:
I can't find any additional information of a "**Meacham**."

———————

Anson Gates Olmstead died on **March 15, 1898**, in Camden, NY. He is buried at the **Forest Park Cemetery**, Camden, Oneida Co., NY.

Around **1862**, **Henry G. Munger** left the employment of **A. G. Olmstead**, traveling to **Cazenovia, Madison County, NY**, where he again found a clerking job in a mercantile store. Here, Henry remained for approx. **two years**.

Author's Notes:
After an extensive search, I am unable to identify the company and/or the person who **Henry** worked for in **Cazenovia, NY**.

———————

About **1864**, Henry left **Cazenovia** and headed to **Syracuse, NY**, where he had accepted a salesman's position in the establishment of "**Edward Price**."

A year later (abt. **1865**), Henry accepted a clerk's position in the mercantile business with the establishment of "**Avery & McCreery**" in **Flint, Michigan**. Here he would remain for **two years**.

Clarence Lucius Avery was born on **July 27, 1835**, at **Cochecton, Sullivan Co., NY**, to **Charles** (1807-1833) and **Clarissa Marvin** (nee **Tayler**) **Avery** (1806-1856).

Clarence married **Flora Mary Hazelton** on **May 14, 1865**, at **Flint, Genesee Co., Michigan**. The couple would have three known children: **Charles Porter Avery** (1865-1916), **Clarence Lucius Avery, Jr.** (1867-1896), and **Mary Louise Avery** (1872-?).

Clarence would go on to partner in the mercantile business with **William Barker McCreery** in **Flint, Michigan**.

William Barker McCreery was born on **July 27, 1836**, at **Mount Morris, Livingston County, NY**, to **Reuben** (1808-1881) and **Susan** (nee **Barker**) **McCreery** (1813-1891).

At the age of two, **1838/39**, William, along with his parents, moved to **Genessee County, Michigan**. He was educated in the common school and at **Nutting's Academy, Lodi, Michigan**.

In **1859/60**, William was admitted to the county bar and practiced law until the American Civil War broke out.

During the **American Civil War**, William enlisted, fighting on the Union side, on **April 23, 1861**, with the rank of sergeant. His first assignment was in **Company F., Second Michigan Infantry**. Later, on **July 10, 1861**, he became a **second lieutenant** commanding the **21st Michigan Infantry**. In a few weeks, on **July 25, 1861**, he was appointed **quartermaster,** and still later, on **Sept. 10, 1861**, he was commissioned **captain** of **Company G**.

William was seriously wounded at **Williamsburg, Virginia,** and at **Chickamauga, GA**. After being wounded at Chickamauga, he was captured by the Confederates. In **1864**, he escaped from **Libby Prison** in **Richmond, Virginia,** after digging a tunnel with the help of other prisoners.

Following the war, in **1864**, William returned home to **Flint, Michigan,** where he engaged in the general merchandise trade of **J. F. Judd**. On **December 14, 1864**, William married **Adeline "Ada" Birdsall Fenton (1838-1884)**, a daughter of **William Matthew (1808-1871)** and **Adelaide S. (nee Birdsall) Fenton**.

The couple would have four known children: **Fenton Reuben McCreery (1866-1940)**, **Adalaide Fenton McCreery (1870-1960)**, **Howard McCreery (1877-?)**, **Katherine Minnie Grace McCreery (1879-1971)**.

At some point, William McCreery went into partnership with **Clarence L. Avery,** forming the firm of the "**Avery** & **McCreedy**" dry goods store in Flint.

Among his many accomplishments, **William B. McCrery** was the founder of **Citizens National Bank** and one of the builders and directors of the **Chicago and Northeastern Railway**. He was also one of the original directors of **Flint Waterworks** and served as **Mayor of Flint** from **1865-66**. He was the **US Collector of Internal Revenue** for the eastern district of Michigan from **1871-74**, served as the **State Treasurer** from **1874-78**, and was a member of the **State Board of Agriculture** from **1882-1890**.

William's wife, **Ada (nee Fenton) McCreery**, died on **February 25, 1884**. Following Ada's death, William married **Genevieve Decker (1849-1899),** in **1885** in **Flint, Michigan**.

William Barker McCreery died on **December 9, 1896**. He is buried at **Glenwood Cemetery**, Flint, Michigan, along with his first wife, **Adeline,** and second wife, **Genevieve**.

In the spring of **1867**, **Henry G. Munger** returned east to **Belleville, Jefferson Co., NY**. On **March 18**, at **Belleville**, he married **Ellen Arvilla Searles**, born in **Ellisburg, Jefferson Co., NY**, on **November 8, 1847**, a daughter of **William Thurston** (1808-1864) and **Lucinda Bicknell** (nee **White**) **Searles** (1826-1901).

William Thurston Searles (H. G. Munger's father-in-law) was born on **June 27, 1808**, in **Jefferson County, NY** to **James Searles** (1769-1847) and **Abigail** (nee **Thurston**) **Searles** (1775-1833).

In **Belleville,** William was educated at the **Union Academy**, a school engaged in what was termed *classical study*, a liberal arts education rooted in ancient history. It was referred to as "Union Academy" because it was never to be ruled by any sect or church denomination. It was a school that belonged to the people.

On **March 12, 1846**, in **Ellisburg Village, Jefferson Co., NY**, **William T. Searles** married **Lucinda Bricknell White,** daughter of **Ward Walton White** (1799-1853) and **Arvilla Bicknell Searles** (1803-1827),

Following their marriage, William and Lucinda lived in Ellisburg Village for a few years and then moved to **Belleville, NY.**

William Thurston and **Lucinda Bricknell Searles** would have eight known children: **Ellen Arvilla Searles** (1847-1924), **Fanna A. Searles** (1848-1909), **Mary William Searles** (1850-1851), **Charles W. Searles** (1852-1918), **Lucia E. Searles** (1854-1854), **Ida Lucinda Searles** (1856-?), **George Walton Searles** (1858-1934) and **James Edward Searles** (1863-?).

For many years, **William T. Searles** was engaged in the **mercantile business**, with stores in both **Ellisburg Village, NY** and **Belleville, NY.**

Ellis Village (Ellisburg Village) is not to be confused with the actual town of **Ellisburg, Jefferson Co., NY.**

Ellisburg Village is a small hamlet or community of roughly 250 people, located near the center of the town of Ellisburg.

In **1895**, Ellisburg Village set itself apart from the town of Ellisburg by incorporating.

In **1872**, William came to **Madison Co., NY,** where he purchased a homestead of 160 acres, which he improved upon.

He later took up the study of law, being admitted to the bar in **1876**.

In the fall of **1877**, William was elected **County Judge** and in **May** of **1881**, he formed a partnership with **Mr. Kelly** in the law firm of **Searles & Kelly**.

At one time, **William T. Searles** was head of a railroad enterprise and other prominent leading business activities in Belleville.

William Thurston Searles died on **May 12, 1864,** and was buried at **Ellisburg Rural Cemetery**, Ellisburg, Jefferson Co., NY. Following his death, his widow, **Lucinda,** moved to **Adams** in **Jefferson Co**. She died there in **January 1901** and is also buried at **Ellisburg Rural Cemetery**.

Henry G. and **Ellen** (nee **Searles**) **Munger**, following their marriage in **Belleville**, moved to Ellis Village (Ellisburg Village), Jefferson Co., NY, a small hamlet located in the town of Ellisburg.

Here **Henry**, eager to go into business for himself, went into a partnership with a **Mr. Sterns** (**1867**) in Ellisburg Village, Jefferson Co., NY, thus establishing the dry goods firm of "**Sterns & Munger**" in a store once owned by Henry's father-in-law, **William Thurston Searles**. A year later (**1868**) Mr. Sterns sold his interest in the business to **Mr. C. L. Avery**, Henry's former employer in Flint, Michigan, who had also come east. The business at Ellisburg Village continued under the name of "**Avery & Munger**."

Henry G. and **Ellen Arvilla** (nee **Searles**) **Munger** would have six known children: **Mabel Irene Munger** (1868-1926), **Bertha Ellen Munger** (1870-1943), **Frederick Searle Munger** (1873-1930), **Mary Elizabeth Munger** (1876-1952), **Frances L.** "**Fanny**" **Munger** (1877-Date unknown), **Alice Dorothy Munger** (1879-1919), and **Bruce Gillette Munger** (1890-1893).

In **1869**, **Avery & Munger**" closed their store in Ellisburg Village, owing to bad credit conditions and other local faults of trade.

Next, the partners headed to **Herkimer, Herkimer Co., NY** and greener pastures.

CHAPTER TWO
AVERY & MUNGER'S HERKIMER DRY GOODS STORE
[The Fox Block, Herkimer, Herkimer Co., NY]
1869 – 1872

Following the closing of their **Avery & Munger's** store in Ellisburg Village in **1869**, the two partners moved part of their stock to **Herkimer, NY**, where they had purchased the dry goods store of **Taylor Brothers** located in the **Fox Block**, just north (to the left) of the **Waverly Hotel** on **North Main Street**.

Fox Block: Around **1864, Charles J. Fox** (1819 – 1884), a **cooper (**a barrel maker**)** and **painter** by trade, had the **Fox Block** constructed. At one time, he owned and managed **the Waverly Hotel**, to the right of his block. He was married to **Mary E.** (nee **Cox**) **Fox** (1823 – 1877). They had two known sons: **Charles Fox** (1845 -?) and **Jabez E. Fox** (1848 – 1897).

According to **H. G. Munger's** obituary, the date that **Avery & Munger** opened their store in Herkimer was **April 1, 1869**.

The Herkimer Democrat & Little Falls Gazette newspaper, dated **May 26, 1869,** ran an advertisement for the newly opened **Avery & Munger's** dry goods store with the headlines: *Avery & Munger Have Re-Opened The New York Store* – "The New York Store" referring to the **Taylor Brothers' New York Store**.

During this period, many dry goods stores throughout **New York State** incorporated the term "**New York Store**" into the name of their firm. It is thought that the term refers to the fact that these stores purchased their goods through buying trips in prestigious **New York City**, America's center for trade and commerce.

It is interesting to note that although the date of **Avery & Munger's New York Store** opening may be in question, throughout the years Munger's has always celebrated the anniversary of their opening during the month of **May**.

Avery & Munger's new store consists of one **17' x 19' room**, lit by the glow of a kerosene lamp and staffed by two salesclerks (besides Avery and Munger).

Avery and Munger's partnership and their store both proved to be short-lived.

The *****Herkimer Democrat & Little Falls Gazette** newspaper, dated **February 28, 1872**, ran a

"Great Clearing Out Sale" ad for the **Avery & Munger's** store to *"Close Out Business,"* with Avery and Munger having decided to dissolve their partnership. *"Everything Must Be Sold Within The Next 30 Days!"* the ad read.

By **May 27, 1872, Clarence L. Avery** had opened his own dry goods store, also in the **Fox Block,** under the name "**C. L. Avery**."

*Author's Notes:
During the late **1860's** and on into the **early 1900's,** there were two distinct Herkimer, NY newspapers that carried ads and articles concerning **H. G. Munger.**

There was the **Herkimer Democrat,** founded in **1848,** which then, in **1869,** merged with the **Little Falls Gazette,** publishing under the dual name of **Herkimer Democrat & Little Falls Gazette.** In **1876,** the **Herkimer Democrat & Little Falls Gazette** became once again the **Herkimer Democrat.**

On **Nov. 1, 1898,** Herkimer's first daily newspaper emerged: **The Evening Telegram.**

In **1904,** the **Herkimer Democrat** ceased publication.

The Evening Telegram continued, eventually taking on the name of **The Herkimer Evening Telegram.**

New York Store,

HERKIMER, N. Y.

AVERY & MUNGER,

HAVE RE-OPENED

THE NEW YORK STORE,

WITH A LARGE AND WELL SELECTED

STOCK OF

DRY GOODS,

CARPETS,

OIL CLOTHS,

&c,

WE SHALL SELL GOODS AT THE

LOWEST PRICES,

FOR CASH ONLY,

AND AT ONE PRICE TO ALL)

ALL GOODS WARRANTED TO BE AS REPRESENTED.

WE SHALL BE PLEASED

TO SHOW GOODS

WHETHER WE SELL OR NOT.

May 12, 1869.

Avery & Munger
New York Store
Herkimer, NY
1st known Advertisement
The Herkimer Democrat &
Little Falls Gazette
May 26, 1869

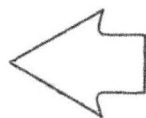

**[Advertisements]
Resized from Originals**

Avery & Munger
New York Store
Herkimer, NY
**Closing Out Business
Partnership Dissolution**
The Herkimer Democrat &
Little Falls Gazette
Feb. 28, 1872

March 1st, 1872.

AVERY & MUNGER,

NEW YORK STORE

HERKIMER, N. Y.

GREAT CLEARING OUT SALE!

---

30 Days!

30 Days!

30 Days!

TO CLOSE OUT THE BUSINESS

FOR CASH ONLY!

Having decided to dissolve partnership, we offer our large stock of

Dry Goods

At a Great Reduction,

and will give

BARGAINS

IN ALL KINDS OF

DRY GOODS!

This is a good opportunity to all who wish to buy goods cheap. The greater portion of this stock

MUST BE SOLD

WITHIN THE

NEXT 30 DAYS!

LOOK OUT FOR BARGAINS!

The Fox Block
North Main Street, Herkimer, NY
[Waverly Hotel far right]
Fox Block to the immediate left of the hotel.
[Postcard resized from original.]

CHAPTER THREE
THE H. G. MUNGER'S NEW YORK STORE
Herkimer, Herkimer Co., NY
[A Timeline of Events Through the Early Years]
1873 – 1899

As mentioned before, following the dissolvement of the **Avery & Munger's** dry goods store partnership in **1872**, H. G. Munger continued to do business at the old stand in the **Fox Block** in Herkimer, now under the business name of **New York Store/H. G. Munger.**

The **Watertown Daily Times,** dated **April 22, 1873**, reported: *Mr. Clark Bull, who has been in the employment of F. Waite & Son for the past three years, the time for which he was hired, has left town for Herkimer, where he is to resume his business with H. G. Munger. He has many good friends who will miss him and whose best wishes attend him. Good luck to you, "Clark."*

Whether Clark Bull and H. G. Munger worked together when Munger partnered in the "**Sterns & Munger's**" dry goods store in Ellisburg Village in **1867** or in **1868** is not known–a time when **Sterns** left the firm and **H. G. Munger** partnered with **C. L. Avery.**

Clark E. Bull was born in **Ellisburg, Jefferson County, NY,** on **August 20, 1848**, to **Crispin Bull** (1812-1884) and **Harriet N**. (nee **Green**) **Bull** (1817-1885).

Clark married **Orphana Adelle "Allie" D. Orr** abt. **1875.**

Adelle was born in **Richland, Oswego, NY,** in **1848** to **Alexander Orr** (1800-1866) and **Elvira Maria** (nee **Chapin**) **Orr** (1810-1878).

Clarence and **Adelle Bull** had two known children: **Clarence Crispen Bull** (1876-1935) and **Florence Orr Bull** (1881-1957).

The **1880 New York State Census** lists **Clark Bull**, 31 yrs. of age, with the occupation of "**Millinery & Fancy Goods Store.**" His wife, listed as "**Alice,**" has the occupation of "**Milliner.**"

Orphana Adelle "Allie" D. (nee **Orr**) **Bull** died in **1896** in **Denver, Colorado**. She is buried at **Fairmount Cemetery, Denver, Colorado.**

Clark E. Bull died **August 22, 1916**, in **Denver, Colorado**. He is also buried at **Fairmount Cemetery.**

The **Herkimer Democrat, March 7, 1877**, reported: *Messrs. Munger and Avery will close their stores from now until the 15th inst. at 7 o'clock p.m. and after that date at 7:30 p.m.*

The **Herkimer Democrat, March 20, 1878**, read, *Mr. H. G. Munger has rented the saloon rooms in the Fox Block and is having them fitted up for a first-class sale and show room for carpets.*

By **March 23rd**, the "**new carpet room**" was open for business.

In that same issue of the **Herkimer Democrat**, **March 20, 1878**, it was reported, *C. E. Bull, who has been clerk for H. G. Munger for a number of years, has gone into business in the same block.*

Clark E. Bull ran a **millinery shop** that sold **women's hats** and **accessories**.

Clarance L. Avery, Munger's former partner, continued his dry goods business, "**C. L. Avery**" until **March** of **1879**.

The **Herkimer Democrat** newspaper, **February 26, 1879**, ran an ad for "**C. L. Avery**" stating that the dry goods store was "**Going Out of Business**," and thus was holding a "**30-Day Close-Out Sale**."

Clarence L. Avery next opened a dry goods store in **West Winfield, Herkimer Co., NY**, where he remained in business for a year.

On **March 12, 1879**, the **Herkimer Democrat** reported, *Our enterprising fellow townsman, Mr. H. G. Munger, has purchased the house and lot on the corner of Mary and Washington Streets, opposite the residence of Hon. A. H. Prescott, and will erect a beautiful and commodious residence the coming season.*

Whether Munger eventually built a house next to the existing house at the corner of Mary and Washington Street in Herkimer is not known. What is known is that in **1880 H. G. Munger** had a home built at **426 North Main Street**, **Herkimer**, which became the family's home in which Munger would live the rest of his life.

The **Herkimer Democrat, June 25, 1879**, reported: *H. G. Munger met with a serious accident Monday night by accidentally falling down the stairs, striking his face and breaking his nose.*

By **March** of **1880,** Avery had returned to Herkimer, where he again opened a dry goods store in the **Fox Block**.

A profile of the home at **426 N. Main St**. appeared in an **Architectural Walking Tour of Herkimer** two-page handout. The tour, taking place on August 27, 2007, showcased thirteen different historical homes (architecturally-wise) in Herkimer.

The profile of the Munger home as it appeared in the handout: *426 North Main Street – H. G. Munger – Zoller – Hanna House Victorian Style – wooden clapboard structure was built in 1880 by Henry G. Munger who at one time owned Munger's Department Store on Main Street in Herkimer. The architect was A. N. Russell, Ilion, NY. It has three stories, 14 rooms, complex pitched roof, entrance porch has ornate detailing, large double-hung doors, inner doors with tinted glass portraying fruit and outer door with tinted glass with flowers. There are dormers, medallions, the sun porch on the left used to be the porch which was used for horse drawn carriages to pull up to the house to drop their passenger(s) off. Notice the lightning rod on the roof. The garage outback has a turntable in it. Today the house is used for apartments and offices.*

The **Herkimer Democrat, December 22, 1880**, reported: *Sheriff D. C. Paine will take possession of the jail on January 1st. W. H. Eaton, now bookkeeper for Mr. H. G. Munger, has made an excellent jailer, and his services have been greatly appreciated by the people of this county.*

The **Herkimer Democrat, May 30, 1883**, states, *Plans have been perfected by Mr. Charles J. Fox for the erection of a brick store on the vacant lot between the bank and the Waverly House. It will have a frontage of 40 feet, with a correspondingly simple depth. When completed, it will be occupied by Mr. H. G. Munger, the popular dry goods merchant.*

At the time, the bank went under the name of "**Herkimer Bank**." Fifteen years later, **1898**, the bank would open its door at the same location as the "**Herkimer National Bank**."

Charles Fox's new building was located to the right of the **Waverly Hotel**, in what was referred to as the "**Bank Block**." The Herkimer Bank stood to the right of the new block. Munger's store in the **Fox Block** was located to the left of the **Waverly Hotel**.

In no time at all, Munger's store in the Bank Block became inadequate. Sometime later, Munger purchased a frame building, which sat next to the **Palmer House Hotel**, from **Charles W. Palmer**, owner of the Palmer House. The building was moved across the street and relocated behind the **Bank Block** adjoining the back of Munger's store. The frame of the building was 22 feet wide and 50 feet long. The first floor of the new addition was occupied with stock of cloaks, curtains and underwear, and the second story with carpets, blankets, oilcloths and surplus stock. The entrance to the frame house add-on from the main store was through a small double doorway supplied with swinging doors, which were covered with tin.

The Argus, an **Albany, NY,** newspaper dated **January 12, 1892,** stated: *Herkimer, Jan. 11: The dry goods store of H. G. Munger was reported robbed this morning. Mr. Munger showed the correspondent a rear window leading to the cellar. "Here is where they got in," said he.*

The window is fastened by an upright bolt. Mr. Munger said the bolt could be shaken out of the socket by rattling the window from the outside.

The door at the head of the cellar steps, a clerk said, had not been kept locked. Mr. Munger said that the thieves carried several trays of jewelry into the cellar and emptied them. They also carried off a number of silk handkerchiefs that retailed for a half dollar.

When asked if any money had been taken, Mr. Munger said that he had not looked to see. The man at the money drawer seemed surprised when asked that question. He said there were five or six dollars left in the drawer and it had not been disturbed. He didn't think the thieves could secure the money unless they knew the finger combination under the drawer. If they attempted it, he said, the bell would ring. Mr. Munger says the class of goods taken would indicate that peddlers wanted them. It is the largest store in town, yet the missing goods are valued at only $150.

In **1897, Charles Porter Avery**, Clarence L. Avery's oldest son, and **Eleazer Kneelan LaDue** went into the dry goods trade in the **Fox Block** in **Herkimer** under the name of "**LaDue & Avery**." Later, "**LaDue & Avery**" would reopen their store in the **Long Shore Block** in Herkimer.

Eleazer Kneelan LaDue was born on **September 24, 1858, Fairfield, Herkimer Co., NY**, a son of **Cephas** (1834-1913) and **Guelma A.** (nee **Phillips**) **LaDue.**

Eleazer married **Adelaide Helen "Addie" Jackson** (1864-1943) in **1884**, Herkimer, NY. She was the daughter of **Daniel** & **Louise Elizabeth** (maiden name unknown) **Jackson.**

Eleazer and **Adelaide** would have one known child, a daughter, **Edna LaDue** (1891-1965).

Eleazer Kneelan LaDue died on **January 5, 1934**, Herkimer, NY. He is buried at the **Oak Hill Cemetery** in Herkimer. Adelaide Helen LaDue died on **April 9, 1943**, in Herkimer. She is also buried at **Oak Hill Cemetery.**

Charles Porter Avery was born on **December 24, 1865, Flint, Genesse Co., Michigan** to **Clarence Lucius** (1835-1906) and **Flora Mary** (nee **Hazelton**) **Avery** (1841-1917).

Charles married **Meribah Small** (born April 1867, **Small's Bush, NY**), daughter of **Jacob Frederick** (1826-1896) and **Ann** (nee **Rankins**) **Small** (1830-1880).

Charles and **Meribah** had two known children, both sons: **Hazelton Small Avery** (1894-1983) and **Clarence Lucius Avery** (1901-1962).

Charles Porter Avery died in **1916** from an acute gastric hemorrhage, while living with his family in **Guaynabo, Puerto Rico**. He is buried at **Oak Hill Cemetery** in Herkimer, NY.

His widow, **Meribah** (nee **Small**) **Avery,** died in **1957** in Herkimer, NY. She too is buried at **Oak Hill Cemetery**.

And then on **Saturday evening, February 26, 1898**, H. G. Munger's store in the **Bank Block** on **North Main Street** became engulfed in flames.

Herkimer First National Bank

[N. E. Corner of N. Main & Green St. Herkimer, NY]

Bank Block to the Left of Bank.

[Postcard Resized from original.]

CHAPTER FOUR
THE HERKIMER FIRE OF 1898
[Occurring on February 26, 1898]

According to a newspaper article in a **Little Falls, NY** newspaper dated **March 1, 1898**: *At 11:45 last Saturday night (**Feb. 26th**), fire was discovered in what was known as the cloakroom of H. G. Munger's store on Main Street. The fire department got to the scene of the fire in good time and soon had four streams playing upon the flames, which were confined to the two-story frame addition attached to the main part of Mr. Munger's store in the rear.*

The Herkimer Bank Block is made of brick, but a few years ago Mr. Munger's business, demanding more floor space, purchased C. W. Palmer's frame building, which then stood on the site of the Palmer House Block, and had it moved to the rear of the Herkimer Bank Block and made it a part of his store.

This frame building was 22 feet wide and 50 feet long, the first story being occupied by Mr. Munger's store with a stock of cloaks, curtains and underwear, and the second story with carpets, blankets, oilcloths and surplus stock.

The value of this stock was about $12,000. The building was worth about $2,500.

This building and stock are a total loss. The entrance to this department from the main store was through a small double doorway supplied with swinging doors, which were covered with tin, and this latter fact prevented the flames from being carried to the main part of the store.

The main part was filled with smoke, however, and this damaged, more or less, the large stock of dry goods and fancy articles carried by Mr. Munger. The firemen, under the direction of Chief Engineer Edward Small, succeeded in confining the fire to the wooden structure. Several large, framed buildings were in close proximity to the fire, to wit: Waverly House, Comfort boarding stables, Fisher's Steam Laundry and the Stimson residence. None felt alarmed. All had confidence in the ability of the firemen to confine the flames to the burning building, and this confidence is not misplaced. The fire, it is thought, originated from the furnace. Mr. Munger's loss is fully covered by insurance.

Shortly following the fire, H. G. Munger re-opened his store at the same location in the **Herkimer National Bank Block**, minus the wooden-structured building that he had previously added to the rear of his store.

H. G. Munger ran an ad in the **March 2, 1898, Herkimer Democrat** newspaper that read, *H. G. Munger, NEW YORK STORE! Herkimer, N. Y. – An Announcement! – Owing to a severe fire that occurred in our store on Saturday night, it has become necessary to close the store for a few days until the losses can be adjusted and the stock put in order for resuming business. The annex, containing the cloak, curtain and underwear departments, was destroyed, and the contents entirely burned or rendered nearly worthless. In the main building the damage is principally from water and smoke, but to what extent it is impossible now to determine.*

A prompt announcement will be made in the papers and by bills of the date of resumption of business, when it may be assumed a special sale will be inaugurated to dispose of the damaged stock.

I want to take the occasion to thank the public for their generous patronage, which I have enjoyed these many years, during which there has never before been a suspension of business, and to express the hope that those who have found our store a satisfactory place to do their trading will be patient for a few days, when we will no doubt be able to offer such inducements as will amply repay for the wait. Yours sincerely, **H. G. Munger**.

The **Richfield Springs Mercury, September 22, 1898**, reported: *Monday morning, the old Herkimer bank opened its doors as the Herkimer National Bank. The bank is one of the oldest in the county, having been established in 1868. A state charter was granted in 1885 and now, after 30 years as a local and state bank, the institution passes under the control of the national government. No change will be made in the officers and rules as to deposit, etc.*

H. G. Munger's carpet department has been removed from Fox Opera House Block to the store formerly occupied by G. P. Munson in the Fox Block. The store has been extensively repaired and presents a very attractive appearance, reported the **Herkimer Democrat, November 16, 1898**.

On **April 20, 1899**, the **Richfield Springs Mercury** reported: *E. L. Jackson, who for a number of years, had been the efficient head of the cloak department and had charge of the advertising of the store of H. G. Munger, has purchased an interest in the business. The firm's name will now be H. G. Munger & Co.*

Edgar Long Jackson (1860 – 1939) was born in **Westfield, Chautauqua Co., NY** in **June 1860**. He married **Nellie Wheeler** (1859 – 1946) in **1888**. The couple had three known children: **Evelyn Jackson** (1881 – 1961), **Harvey W. Jackson** (1890 – 1962) and **Charles Irving Jackson** (1893 – 1952). Before coming to Herkimer, NY to work for **H. G. Munger**, Edgar had worked for the **E. C. Tower** store in **Troy, NY**. Edgar died on **December 12, 1939**, in **Albany, NY**. He is buried at the **West Winfield Cemetery**, Herkimer Co., NY.

The Earl Block – Masonic Temple Block – Graves Block:

In **1899**, the new four-story **Earl Block** was erected at the **southeast corner** of **North Main** and **Green Street**, in Herkimer. Here Mr. Munger promptly rented its largest storefront.

An article in the **Herkimer Democrat, May 10, 1899**, stated *The New York Store – H. G. Munger & Co. Have a Fine Display of Goods – There are many things that contribute to the growth and prosperity of a town, village, or city, but the most prominent factor, of which we can imagine is live, energetic businessmen. Herkimer has a full quota of them, and prominent and foremost we find the large department store of H. G. Munger & Co. now occupying their mammoth store in the new Earl building.*

We say mammoth store and mean it, for it is second to none in Central New York. On invitation, the Democratic man was shown through all the departments, and it is simply amazing that Herkimer has such a complete and up-to-date store.

Within its enclosure there are 15,000 square feet of floor space, and the show windows are the largest between Buffalo and New York, being 12 feet 8 inches by 10 feet 8 inches. The carpet room is especially adapted to displaying their elegant line of goods, being 70 by 46 feet, and having 18 large windows, thus providing elegant light, which is essential.

This week, they are having their formal opening. The interior of the store has been especially decorated for the occasion by an experienced trimmer who has shown much excellent taste and artistic ability.

The decorations are principally pink and white, intermingled with evergreens and palms. Adding to this are many beautiful decorative combinations of fabrics taken from their extensive stocks, all of which are most pleasing.

The carpet room on the 2nd floor is filled to overflow, with carpets, rugs, etc. The claim that they have a larger stock than the combined stores in Herkimer County seem to be well substantiated. Their display windows are certainly worth a visit of many miles to inspect. The south window is filled with dainty wash fabrics wrought into paisley shapes and curious designs, showing forcibly that an artistic hand can make from even the most inexpensive material combinations most fascinating. In the north window is displayed a beautiful assortment of fancy silks and dress goods. The quality of these is easily discernible, as one can readily see that only the rich, lustrous materials would stand close examination under such a strong light as these are displayed.

However, these are assuredly most beautified and go far to convince one that there is no need to go elsewhere for the finer and exclusive materials for the adornment of the fair sex.

Each afternoon, from 2:00 p.m. to 5:00 p.m. and 7:30 to 9:30, Wires Orchestra was present to entertain the many visitors. Monday evening, the crowd was immense, and we predict for this enterprising firm a season of unprecedented business.

Shortly after the **Earl Block** opened in **1899**, the dry goods firm of "**LaDue & Avery**" occupied a storefront on the building's **Green Street** side.

CHAPTER FIVE
THE BEGINNING OF A NEW CENTURY
[Expanding the H. G. Munger & Co. Store – The H. G. Munger's Big Store]

In **1903**, H. G. Munger occupied all available space in the **Earl Block**. This was the start of his **big store.**"

The **Observer Dispatch, Utica, NY, January 13, 1904**, reported: *The firm of H. G. Munger & Co., dry goods merchants, which occupies the larger store in the Earl Block, has made arrangements to occupy the ground floor of the adjoining Masonic Temple, which will be completed in April, and also the basement of the building, each 118 feet deep by 59 feet front. The two buildings will be connected by arches and operate together. The two stores together will equal the floor area of a five-story building at 150 by 118 feet.*

On **April 1, 1904**, H. G. Munger & Co. took possession of the ground floor and basement of the newly built **Masonic Temple Block** (to the right of the Earl Block).

The **Herkimer Democrat** reported on **Wednesday, April 6, 1904**, *Important Change – H. G. Munger & Co. Purchase The La Due & Avery Stock* – *H. G. Munger & Co. have purchased the La Due & Avery Department Store adjoining the New York Store in the new Earl Block. The sale took place Friday night and was made public Saturday.*

The New York Store, with its recent addition, the ground floor and basement of the Masonic Temple Block, will have the largest store of any firm in any place of the size of Herkimer in the state.

The business was started by E. K. LaDue in the Fox Block in 1897. Two years later, C. P. Avery (Charles Porter Avery, son of H. G. Munger's former partner Clarence L. Avery) came into the firm, and the business was moved to larger quarters in the Long Shore Block.

When the Earl Block was finished (1899), the store was moved to its present location in the Earl Block. Both Mr. LaDue and Avery are of the best men in the community, and their departure from the business field will be regretted by all.

Mr. LaDue will remain with H. G. Munger & Co. and manage the department made by their purchase of this stock. The store was closed for inventory on Monday, and at the end of the month, the stock will be moved to the basement of the store in the Masonic Temple Block. Mr. Avery is to move with his family to Puerto Rico. Avery, along with H. G. Munger, Clarence Dwyer, E. L. Jackson,

E. K. LaDue, and H. H. Longstaff, have an orange grove of 75 acres that will soon commence Bearing, and Mr. Avery is to assume personal control of that business. All will regret the removal of Mr. Avery from Herkimer.

On **Thursday, May 19ᵗʰ, 1904**, Mungers expanded his business into the newly built **Masonic Temple Block** in Herkimer with a **grand opening** celebration.

The **Herkimer Democrat, May 21, 1904**, ran a **H. G. Munger & Co. New York Store** ad with the headline, ***Come to the Opening of the Big New Store – Thursday, Friday and Saturday, May 19ᵗʰ, 20ᵗʰ and 21ˢᵗ***.

New Phone System read a small ad in the **Herkimer Democrat, June 29, 1904**. The article stated: ***H. G. Munger & Co. Install Labor Saving Device*** *– The firm of H. G. Munger & Co. yesterday closed a contract with the telephone system here for the installation in their big store of a private switchboard and intercommunication system. Ten phones will be installed on their private inside line, and communication can be had instantly between any parts of the store's various departments. The system will be a great convenience and time saver.*

In **September** of **1904**, the old **Fox Block**, located directly to the left of the Waverly Hotel where H. G. Munger started out in business in Herkimer back in **1869**, was razed to make way for the new **Hemstreet Block**. The **Herkimer Democrat, September 21, 1904**, reported: *The scaffolding has been removed from the Hemstreet Apartment Block, and the block is one of the prettiest in Herkimer.*

The Great Herkimer Flood of 1910 occurred on **February 28, 1910**, due to the giant blocks of ice and freezing water that were choking the West Canada Creek, causing the creek to break out of its banks and flood portions of **Herkimer, NY**. The **H. G. Munger & Co**. store was spared.

The headlines of **The Utica Observer, March 4, 1910**, read, ***Herkimer Surmounts Her Bewildering Destruction. Crews Cleaning Up Ice-Filled Streets – Mills and Factories of the Village Preparing to Resume Operations Early Next Week – Property Losses Enormous***.

The article went on to say, in part: *Normal conditions are fast being restored in this village. The water is fast receding and the work of restoration is now progressing with considerable speed.* ***Horrocks and Gem Companies Big Losers*** *– Conditions are not so favorable at the factory of the Horrocks Desk Company, which got the first overflow of waters from the creek, or at the mill of the Royal Gem Company, where the walls of the engine room were torn out by the flood.*

H. G. Munger, president of the Horrocks Desk Company (also president of H. G. Munger & Co.), said today that an effort was being made to get the factory running at the earliest opportunity, but a definite time could not be set. A few men are being employed at the factory now.

On **March 2nd, 1910**, the **Herkimer Village Board**, presided over by **President Grogan**, met to discuss the flood situation. One topic discussed was that of furnishing relief to families cut off from supplies. President Grogan then formed a **Citizens Relief Committee**, appointing as one of its members **H. G. Munger**.

In late **March** of **1910**, H. G. Munger & Co. purchased the **Graves Block** to the right of where the Masonic Temple was located and **Judge Grave's home** to the right of the Graves Block.

An article in the **Richfield Springs Mercury, March 24, 1910**, read: *H. G. Munger is building out the Judge Graves residence on Main Street in line with and to the right of the Graves Block and will make the first floor into a shoe store which will be used for the shoe department of the New York Store.*

The room vacated in the big Munger store will be added to the cloak and suit department.

Author's Notes:
An old postcard shows a one floor storefront extension to the right of the **Graves Block** with the name "**H. G. Munger & Co. Shoe Store**" across its entrance. In the background of the extension you can see the Judge Graves residence.

————————

An interesting article on **Munger's** appeared in the **April 13, 1911** edition of the **Richfield Springs Mercury** newspaper. ***They Come From Utica*** – *Few realize how widely spread is the patronage of H. G. Munger & Co.'s Department Store. All know that it is the central trading place of Herkimer County but the business is by no means limited to the Mohawk Valley; from the east as far as Amsterdam and from the length of the Herkimer-Oneonta trolley they come to Herkimer for their dry goods.*

Rome and Utica contribute very substantially to the business of the store while the mail order business extends throughout the state. One day last week, during the opening of a big store in Utica and when many special sales were in progress, a resident of Utica came to Herkimer to Munger & Co., and the bill of goods purchased included 30 pairs of blankets, 20 bed spreads, 49 pairs of curtains, 81 window shades, 31 rugs, 88 yards of linoleum and 200 yards of cotton.

The customer came to Herkimer for these goods, after shopping through the Utica stores and purchased them here because he could do better than at home.

This incident explains why the store has built up a business requiring 125 clerks and has a range of patronage probably wider than any store in the state. – Herkimer Citizen.

The clerks at H. G. Munger & Co.'s store held a twilight picnic last evening at Mirror Lake. Supper was served following of which boat rides and games were enjoyed, reported The **Utica Observer**,

July 13, 1913.

The **Richfield Springs Mercury, June 11, 1914,** read: *The H. G. Munger & Co. store at Herkimer will hereafter be opened only one evening a week, Saturday, until 10 o'clock, thus closing on Monday evenings, beginning June 15th. The store will be open every day at 8:30 a.m. and close at 6 p.m., except Saturdays, and the salespeople are allowed one hour and ten minutes for lunch.*

*A **June 29, 1914,** newspaper clipping read: Main Street swarmed with ladies today between the trolley station and the Munger company store, where the annual nine-cent sale opened. No rain, hail or mud can stop the fair sex when bargains are in sight. A woman will buy more for a dollar than a man can for ten. The trolley cars are crowded and it would be appreciated by the shoppers and others who come to the village if the trolley company would make a slight fill where the cars stop so that it would not be necessary to step out into the mud when alighting from a car in wet weather.*

A large picture of E. L. Jackson, vice president of H. G. Munger & Co. was presented Friday night at the Baptist Church by five of Mr. Jackson's fellow members of the church board and trustees. The occasion was the annual roll call of the church, after a dinner attended by 200 members of the church. Mr. Jackson is one of the oldest trustees of the church and one of the most liberal. The other trustees are Dr. E. G. Kern, George W. Aan, William Ownes, E. P. Sharpe and Owen Williams, reported the **Richfield Springs Mercury, March 9, 1916**.

MAIN STREET, HERKIMER, N. Y.

L to R
Earl Block – Masonic Temple – Graves Block
[Starting at the corner of N. Main & Green St. going south.]
North Main St. Herkimer, NY
Notice Munger's Shoe Store far right.
[Postcard Resized from original.]

Herkimer, New York Flood
March 1st, 1910
Mohawk Street, Herkimer
[Picture taken from Wikimedia Commons Free Media Repository online]

Continued on next page.

The 1910 Herkimer, New York Flood
[caption]
The Dizzy House
Herkimer, N.Y., Flood, 1910
[Picture taken from The 'Real" Herkimer, NY website.]

CHAPTER SIX
THE INFAMOUS HERKIMER FIRE OF 1917
[Occurred on February 9, 1917 - Downtown Herkimer]

H. G. Munger continued to do business in the **Earl Block**, the neighboring **Masonic Block and the Graves Block** next door, until the infamous **Herkimer Fire.** This fire occurred on **February 9, 1917,** at 7:30 in the morning from an explosion in the basement of **Munger's** store. The Herkimer Fire Department, along with the Little Falls and Utica fire departments, helped put out the fire.

Besides the **Earl Block**, the **Masonic Temple** next door was totally destroyed. This temple was where Munger also had stock and did business in the **entire first floor** and **basement** and in **one half of the second floor.** Later the remains of these two buildings would be razed.

The **Graves Block**, however, survived, and **Munger's Shoe Store** continued doing business there for a short period of time.

Other businesses that were affected by the fire were the **First National Bank** and the **Grange Temple**, located on **Green St.**, which also housed The **Evening Telegram** newspaper, **law offices** and **other professional offices** and **apartments.**

It has been reported that one of the large safes located in the **H. G. Munger & Co.** store was opened after the fire. Here the store's inventory, which had been taken only a few days earlier, along with store ledgers, was found undamaged. The information contained in the inventory and ledgers helped the various insurance companies to properly assess the damage, which was later estimated at **half a million dollars**.

Below are several other interesting **dated but not identified** newspaper clippings concerning **Munger's** and the fire:

February 12, 1917, *The H. G. Munger Co. May Soon Resume – This morning the former employees of H. G. Munger & Co., who lost their big department store in the fire, received checks covering their pay. Accompanying the enclosure was a letter in which each one was thanked for their past loyalty and co-operation, and the company expressed a regret that they will be unable to reopen for some time, but Mr. Munger was desirous to talk to them all, and each employee has been requested to make an appointment with him. While no direct statement yet has come from anyone in authority, it is believed and hoped that the store will soon resume its business under* *the best possible circumstances.*

February 14, 1917, *Was Helping Himself* – *Since yesterday afternoon men in the employ of the H. G. Munger Co. have been removing bales of dry goods from the fire ruins on North Main Street where the Munger store formerly stood. Some of the bales and bolts of cloth were so badly damaged that they were useless. Others were not in such bad shape.*

At 5:50 this morning, Officer Moshier saw a man making away with some of the goods under his arm. The officer got the man and discovered that he was Chas Breen of North Washington Street; he had a big roll of cowling under his arm. Charles was locked up, and when arraigned this morning in police court, he pleaded guilty and was sentenced to ten days in jail or paying a fine of $5. He paid the fine.

February 23, 1917, *Encouraging Mr. Munger – Little Falls Citizens Anxious to See New Home Built For Herkimer Department Store* – *Today's Little Falls Times says that the all-important question as to whether H. G. Munger will re-establish in Herkimer his large department store which was destroyed by fire two weeks ago today is as yet undetermined. Little Falls citizens are anxious to see Mr. Munger resume business, it is understood, and are encouraging him to take that view of the matter. It is felt by many that the name which Mr. Munger has established for himself in the mercantile world is one which should be perpetuated through his resumption of business.*

Following the fire, through an arrangement with ex-mayor and men's clothing store owner **T. M. Grogan**, Munger was able to relocate his store, occupying one half of the ground floor space of the **T. M. Grogan** clothing store block, on **North Main St.**, Herkimer. This store block also housed the **Grand Opera House** on its top floor., along with additional first floor space in the same block.

The **Richfield Springs Mercury, March 1, 1917**, reported: *Announcement was made Tuesday that H. G. Munger & Company, the backbone of Herkimer's retail business, which was destroyed by the fire, will be resumed in the near future. H. G. Munger stated that plans that have been developing for some time have successfully materialized and the announcement is a source of gratification to everyone in Herkimer.*

The Munger Company is to occupy one-half of the Grand Opera House Block through an arrangement with ex-mayor T. M. Grogan, who will divide one-half of the ground floor space of his large clothing store for this purpose.

The Munger store will also occupy a large portion of the first floor of the same block. The work of re-establishing the firm will be rushed and is expected that it will be again ready for business by October 1st.

Mr. Munger is to be highly commended for his public-spirited action in re-establishing a business that means so much to the village when, at his age, after a full span of years in service, he might easily have been justified in retiring.

In a newspaper clipping dated **May 8, 1917** (source not given), it was revealed that H. G. Munger would set about to build a totally new store on his Main Street property, located between the **Graves Block** and the **Grand Opera House Block (Grogan Block)**.

The undisclosed newspaper reported: ***New Munger Store Coming – Herkimer's Veteran Merchant Captain to Put Modern Structure on His Main Street Site Between Grand Opera House Block and Graves Building – Will Use Whole Block For His Business***. *A decided flurry of pleased surprise pervaded Herkimer today as the news spread through the business section that Munger's store, the big department house in a small city that has for years been frequented from throughout the valley and beyond, and is known in all parts of Central New York, is to have a rebirth.*

It will literally rise from its ashes, for it will be just three months tomorrow since the splendid, newly stocked emporium that was, sank swiftly to embers. The ambers were not cold when H. G. Munger, like the sterling veteran he is, responded to the enterprising spirit that animates him as in the past, and desirous of standing by his community as it has by him, began planning to establish the "big store" once more.

Resumption of business was promptly affected, thanks to the fraternity and public spirit of T. M. Grogan, who gave part of his handsome new business quarters for the purpose.

Now it is announced that Mr. Munger is about to raise a new block on his own adjoining property just north of the Grogan Store and extending to the Graves Block.

The structure now occupying that site will be razed and upon the 66 by 200-foot site will go up a reinforced concrete block, fully fireproof and modern in every detail. Whether it will be of two or three stories in height is not fully determined at this writing, but one of the features will be a mezzanine floor or gallery-like structure running about the interior between the first and second stories. This will vastly enhance the effect of the store, making for loftiness and better lighting.

There will be elevator equipment and whatever would serve to make the building a completely up-to-date one for its purpose.

It will be wholly occupied by the business. The contract is already let to a Syracuse firm and work is to begin at once. Mr. Munger has general congratulations on his pluck and ever youthful progressiveness, now soon to make the "New York Store" a more notable enterprise than ever before.

The newly built **H. G. Munger & Co**. store also incorporated the "**Graves Block**," which H. G. Munger purchased in **March 1904**. Before construction on the new Munger's store began, however, Judge Graves' home was razed.

Although the **Graves Block** was integrated into the design of Munger's new building, it is not known whether the one floor extended storefront (where the shoe store was located) to the left of the three-story **Graves building**, was razed or incorporated into the new building's design.

Announcement of
H. G. Munger & Co.

We are pleased to inform our many friends and patrons that we will again be open for business in a short time.

Through the courtesy of Mr. T. M. Grogan we have secured the north half of the ground floor in the Opera House Block and part of the second floor for Temporary Quarters.

Our buyers are now in New York combing the market for everything of the latest design and pattern, so that all departments will again be represented by the very best merchandise that can be selected. We will start building our new store as soon as plans are completed.

H. G. MUNGER & CO.
HERKIMER, N. Y.

Richfield Springs Mercury
March 8, 1917
[Resized from Original]

The Way It Was

CLAIMED BY FIRE — Seventy years ago the principle business section and the heart of the county seat's shopping area was leveled by flames. The date was Feb. 9, 1917, and the building shown above was the New York Store, owned and operated by Henry G. Munger. Later, it became known statewide as Munger's Department Store and many of its employees are residents of Herkimer. The fire also destroyed the Grange Hall and the initial home of the Evening Telegram, then on Green Street. (Photo from H. Paul Draheim's collection)

Date Unknown

CHAPTER SEVEN
H. G. MUNGER'S BIG STORE REOPENS ANEW
[May 22, 1918]

On **May 22, 1918**, **H. G. Munger's** new store officially opened for business on **North Main St.** in **Herkimer, NY**.

The new Munger's building, consisting of a **lower level** (basement) and **two upper floors**, was said to have been a modern up-to-date **fireproof** structure, measuring **sixty-six** by **two hundred feet** and built at a cost of **$150,000**.

It had **freight** and **passenger elevators**, a **sprinkler system**, **steel fireproof window sashes** and **wire re-enforced glass**.

The fixtures in the new store were made of **rich mahogany** and all metal fixtures were finished in **statuary bronze**.

That day, **May 22nd**, prior to the grand opening (re-opening), the employees at the Munger's store presented **H. G. Munger** with a beautiful silver loving cup bearing the inscription "**Presented to Henry Gillette Munger by the employees of H. G. Munger & Company in token of their esteem and as a tribute to him as a master merchant. May 22, 1918.**" The presentation was made by **E. L. Jackson**, vice president of the company, on behalf of its employees.

An article in a newspaper clipping (name of newspaper not listed) dated **May 21, 1918,** reads: *Formal Opening of New Munger Store* - *The splendid new Munger & Co. department store will begin its formal opening tomorrow evening. Music for the occasion to be furnished by Perry's orchestra. While many friends have more or less familiarized themselves with the new block and its contents, that have arisen from fire destruction, to be a monument to the Munger spirit of enterprise, any who have not done so should seize this special occasion to appreciate an emporium which in completeness and quality is excelled by none. During the balance of the week following the opening, its gala character is to be continued in a great celebration sale which the management plans to make a noteworthy event full of rare opportunity. The opening concert will be from 7 to 9.*

Herkimer's big store read the headline of an article on Munger's new store opening (source not known). The article is dated **May 23, 1918**.

The article goes on to state, in part: ***Description of the Mercantile Palace That Has Been Created by the Enterprise of a House Almost Fifty Years Before the People – Intimate View Gives Fuller Conception of How Vast the Distance Between Up-to-Date Department Store of the Present and the Modest Beginning of H. G. Munger & Co.***

The official opening last evening of the new store of H. G. Munger & Company marked without doubt the most impressive event in the mercantile history of the Mohawk Valley. The occasion, bringing together as it does the present, past and future, demonstrates through the medium of a great department store the result of industry, perseverance and business integrity covering nearly half a century.

The constructive policy on which the success of this concern has been based, is particularly in evidence at the present time, when a building of the type opened Wednesday evening has been erected and completed in the face of the very unusual obstacles which have retarded work of this nature during the past year.

The new Munger store is as nearly fireproof and vermin-proof as modern engineering, science and skill can make it.

"Monolithic" as if cut from "one rock" the building stands, covering a ground area of 200 x 66 ft., two stores and basement in height.

The construction from coping wall to foundation is of reinforced concrete frame made up of heavy columns with massive capital supporting the flat slab floors without the aid of unsightly beams. This frame was literally cast in a mold of wood, over 150,000 feet of lumber being used to form the mold. Upon the formwork was laid a network of over one hundred tons of small steel bars before the concrete was poured.

Mechanical equipment included complete heating apparatus, freight and passenger elevators, wiring and power lines, sprinkler system and plumbing complete in every detail. A sprinkler system, the most approved type protects each floor, and is equipped with a street alarm. Further fire protection is afforded by the installation of the most modern type of steel fireproof windows sash and wire reinforced glass throughout the entire building.

One of the special features of the store is a large central stairway of special design leading from the first floor to the basement. High stories in proportion to the length of the rooms permit remarkably fine ventilation.

The lighting of a dry goods store is a matter requiring unusual care, and many types of lighting fixtures were considered before a decision was reached. Pear-shaped Monax glass globes were finally selected as meeting the conditions and the soft, evenly diffused light meets all the requirements. The new store also ranks among the "daylight" stores which are finding such favor with the public, all-glass construction being used wherever possible and an abundance of light permits patrons to make selections of merchandise and match colors with a feeling of perfect security.

The walls are ivory tinted throughout the store, and the elevator enclosures and enclosed stairways are finished in gilt, a happy contrast to the usual dark finish.

The fixtures, of a rich mahogany finish throughout, are the last word in department store equipment. Wall and show cases, tables and counters were all especially designed for the Munger store in conformance with what is conceded to be best adapted for department store use.

Beauty and harmony of finish have been sought and found, but no money has been wasted in idle show. All metal fixtures are finished in statuary bronze which blends harmoniously with the mahogany furnishings. There is no gaudy elaboration anywhere, as little inside as out. The beauty of the new store is the beauty of simple elegance, harmony of proportion, excellence of arrangement. For all it is so big it will be found to be singularly cozy and comfortable. There is no cold grandeur about Munger's.

One of the most interesting features connected with the new store is the modern show windows. With a building 66 ft. in width, a window frontage of nearly 150 feet has been secured, with a wide, spacious entrance - this added display space being secured by what is termed an arcade front.

While Munger & Company make it a point to keep their windows always well attractively trimmed, they are attracting special interest in their present holiday dress, an electric fountain serving as the center of attraction in the island window, the other window also being dressed in a particularly attractive manner. Added display space is obtained by the second story show windows which occupy the entire width of the store front.

Throughout the store there are palms, boxwood trees and spring blossoms of many kinds, interspersed with merchandise attractively displayed; they find an ideal background in the ivory-tinted walls and columns. The special opening attraction, a miniature of a battlefield in France, near the city of Verdun, is placed on the second floor, where it will remain on exhibition during the opening days.

The store is equipped with the most modern type of pneumatic tube system operated by a ten-horsepower G. E. centrifugal exhaust set. Installation required approximately 24,000 feet of coated turned steel and aluminum tubing, with terminals at central office and dispatching stations finished in statuary bronze.

There is also installed an Auto-Call system known as the "mechanical finder of men." With this system the heads of departments can be speedily located in any part of the building and summoned to answer telephone calls or confer with customers.

Proof of the extraordinary care and intelligence exercised in the construction of the new building is found in the mastic flooring, which gives a uniform surface similar to the finest grade of linoleum. It is noiseless, fireproof, elastic, and absolutely sanitary, qualities that make instant appeal to both customer and employee, whose comfort was the chief consideration in deciding the use of this high-grade flooring.

Employees are provided with the latest type of resting stool, placed at the back of the counters, and individual sanitary steel lockers for each employee are located in the basement.

The store is manned by an organization trained to the ninth power in the selection and purchase of merchandise, whose powers are supplemented and extended by membership in a New York syndicate and affiliation with National Association of Dry Goods Merchants.

Through such means as these, they are constantly supplied with data and accurate information as to the exact state of the markets, furnishing them with an accurate and scientific basis as to when to buy and what to buy.

Substantial financial backing enables them to purchase the right merchandise at the right time, at the right price and in such quantities as their judgement dictates.

Munger & Company back their buyers as they do their customers, and this unrestricted backing has won and held men of courage, keenness, and exceptional business ability, whose co-operative work is marked by a spirit of friendly rivalry as to which shall offer to the store's patrons the best merchandise and the best service.

But the man whose business sagacity has formed the cornerstone of this successful concern is H. G. Munger, endowed with a keen commercial sense with broad vision and unusual courage in the face of difficulties. He has again and again, during his business career, faced situations which would have meant defeat to one of less strength of character. The fire of February 1917 seemed the crowning blow, but out of that disaster has come a bigger and a better store. It would seem a time to rest content with the work accomplished, but the progressive spirit of the mast merchant is expressed by Mr. Munger in his statement that but the foundation has been laid.

It is a foundation, broad and true. That the structure reared upon it may continue to grow and expand in a manner worthy of its founder and of its past reputation is a wish that finds an echo in the hearts of many in the Mohawk Valley.

Artist's Rendering of the
New H. G. Munger & Co. Department Store
North Main Street, Herkimer, NY
Grand Opening
Held on Wednesday May 22, 1918

H. G. Munger & Co.
Grand Opening Celebration
Opened Wednesday Evening May 22, 1918, for Inspection
Grand Celebration Sale
Thursday, Friday and Saturday, May 23, 24 & 25th.
(Exact Date and Publication Unknown)
Full Page Newspaper Advertisement – Resized to Fit Page
...Transcription of Ad on Following Page...

Transcription of the Main Body of the Mungers New Store Opening Advertisement

H. G. Munger & Co.
Forty-eight Years of Service
1300 Sq. Ft In 1869 – 42,000 Sq. Ft. In 1918

You Are Cordially Invited To Attend Our
Grand Opening Celebration of the Completion of Our New Store
Open Wednesday Evening, May 22nd, for Inspection
Music by Perry's Full Orchestra
Great Celebration Sale Thursday, Friday and Saturday
May 23rd, 24th and 25th

Our New Store – Your Store

"Just down the street," a stone's throw in the matter of distance, but farther, much in service – a move to a store building that realizes our ambition of service – a store built up to carry out the ideas and ideals which have always been ours. But at heart the same store, a store whose creed is satisfaction and faith (next part of sentence is missing). The same (word missing) a store built up by 48 years of value giving, fairness, broadness, honesty and satisfaction (rest of sentence missing).

Larger? Yes! Finer? Yes! But still the same store in our determination to let you be the judge and jury of your own satisfaction. Our earnest appreciation is extended to you. Were it not for your encouragement and your help, this magnificent structure would not have been built – were it not for your interest and advice this handsome mercantile establishment would not have been achieved.

After the fire of February 9th, 1917, when the demand for the re-establishment of our store became insistent, when the people of the broad community who had been served by us for years, raised their voices and demanded THEIR STORE. The grave aspect of the times, local conditions, and the peculiar building difficulties of the day were given due consideration, and the announcement that a store would be built was made only after it had been decided that a store worthy of the confidence and pride of our community would be erected.

Our feeling as we near the culmination of our operation is one of relief, not at all anxiety, for we know what we have built is good. When so large a part of the world is engaged in the destruction of property, there is an added pleasure in substantial constructive work of this kind. A much cheaper store could have been built that would have housed our business but makeshifts are foreign to the (word(s) unreadable) policy of H. G. Munger & Co. – foreign to the policy upon which the success of this concern is based. We have no fear as to the results. The results are in your hands, and as we built this store, at your command, we are content to let them rest there. But, after all, the point of real importance is not how fine a store this is, but how good a store it is to be. The store will perpetuate the spirit of the reception accorded it and reply by its ability in serving.

The traditions, the customs, the atmosphere of the old store – Munger's you regarded so highly, Munger's treasured memory – will be revived, but on a scale that means more to you than we can properly describe.

The great war has given us all a new understanding of our money and the economy of our money: it has made us desire to spend less money, but rather to get more out of the money we do spend.

This principle, then, is the cornerstone of the policy of our new store. The buying power of your dollar is now increased – tomorrow – next week – and forever after.

Your Indulgence Is Asked For Any Overcrowding There May be On Our Opening Days.

PNEUMATIC TUBES

On this page and the next I have pictured three different views of the same **pneumatic tube** (cylindrical carrier) which was once used (along with dozens of others) in **Munger's** department store back in the day.

The pneumatic system worked as follows to process a customer's sale:

The Clerk would twist the tube (carrier) to open it, put the customer's sales slip and payment in it, then twist the tube the opposite way to close it. Next, the clerk placed the tube in a portal which, through forced air transported the tube, through a network of tubing, to the money room where it was processed. The tube was then sent back with the sales receipt stamped "paid" and any change which the customer had coming to them. These portals were located in each department of the store (on each floor).

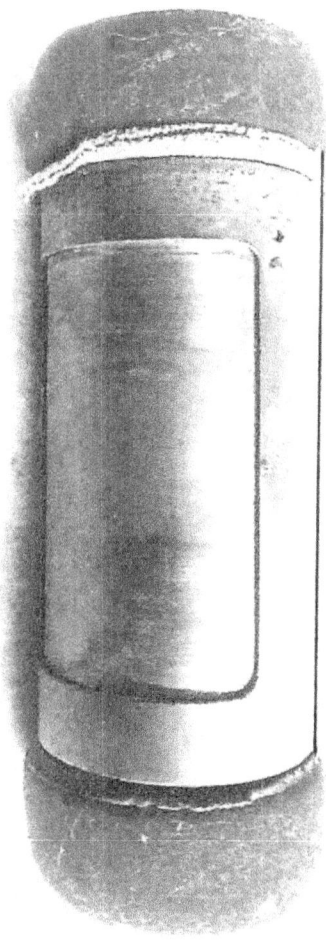

Photographs
Have Been Resized
from Originals.

Continued on next page.

Photograph
Has Been Resized
from Original.

Author's Notes:

The Pneumatic Tube System (cash carrying system) mentioned above was invented by William Murdock in the 1780's. By the mid 1880's the system was used in the finest department stores in America. In 1918, Munger's installed such a system.

This system eliminated the need for cash registers to ring up sales and make change for customers. Now the customer's sales slip and cash payment were placed in a metal tube, which could be twisted open and shut. The tube was then placed in a chute. These chutes were prominently located in each department of the store. Then by pneumatic suction, the tube was sent to the cash office. The tube, including change and the customer's paid receipt, was then returned in the same manner. When a customer looked up, they would see the entire ceiling filled with tubing throughout the store, all leading to the cash office.

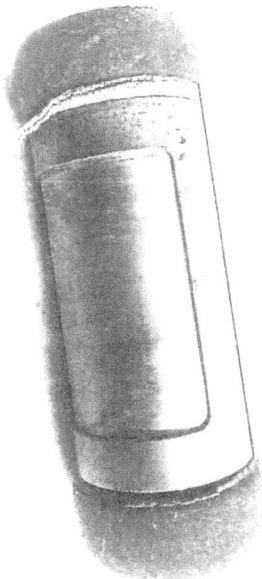

A Picture of An Actual Pneumatic Tube
Once Used in Munger's
[Photo has been resized from Original]

CHAPTER EIGHT
THE H. G. MUNGER & CO. 50ᵀᴴ ANNIVERSARY

[Celebrated June 7th to June 16th, 1919.]

A year after the opening of its new department store, in **1918,** Munger's once again celebrated another milestone in **1919**. This time it was for the **golden anniversary** of the founding of **H. G. Munger & Co**.

The **anniversary celebration** and storewide sale ran from **June 7ᵗʰ** to **June 16ᵗʰ, 1919**.

An article from the **Herkimer Citizen, June 10, 1919**, reported:

————

His Golden Anniversary
H. G. Munger Completes Fifty
Years' Business Service
In Herkimer

————

Splendid Reception Marked the Event Friday Evening
When Thousands of Friends Extended Congratulations
On the Newest Achievement – The Modest Store of 1869
Becomes One of the Great Department Stores of the State
-The Greatest Business Event in the History of Central New York

————

Golden Anniversaries of any kind are rare, but the one celebrated in Herkimer on Friday evening by H. G. Munger & Company, who this year are rounding out 50 years in the retail dry goods business, was particularly unique in many ways. Perhaps the most prominent feature of the event was the whole-hearted participation of the store's public, not only Herkimer alone but every town for miles around. It was a community event not in a limited geographical sense, but in the sense that the participants were those when the Earl Block was completed and Munger moved into the largest store space therein. It was considered a notable business expansion.

But the dynamic force within clamored for greater expansion, for more space to carry more merchandise to meet the needs of more and more customers. This needed space was obtained when the new Masonic Block was erect in which H. G. Munger & Co. leased all the storage space available. Although it appeared roomy at first this store too, soon proved inadequate, and plans were under consideration for enlarging it when the disastrous fire of 1917 wiped out both the Earl and the Masonic Block, leaving Munger's and many other of Herkimer business houses homeless.

Mr. Munger is an optimist. Remarkable courage was a prominent attribute to the boy of 20, who had embarked in business in the old Fox Block in 1869, and that courage still marks the man of 70, who looked at the smoking ruins of a business that it had taken 48 years to build up. With large interests and several manufacturing and financial institutions, and the time having come when the mere making of money was no longer an object, the natural course would have been to terminate a long and honorable business career by retiring from the active field. But local sentiment in Herkimer County was very much against the discontinuance of the Munger store and yielding to the insistent demand. Mr. Munger, with indomitable courage and in the face of the very unusual obstacles presented in the spring of 1917, announced his intention to build a new store, and the present structure, which was opened a year ago, was the result. Having decided to build, nothing short of the best was considered, and the building erected is of a type in keeping with what the institution stands for, substantial, modern in every detail of finish and equipment, and so constructed as to take care of the future expansion of the business.

It has been said that most successful big-business enterprises in existence today owe their success in almost every case, not to modern systems and efficient engineering, but to the strong, virile personality of some individual leader. No better example of this can be found than the department store of H. G. Munger & Co. Mr. Munger has so stamped the business with his personality that it is ineradicable, and to his personal characteristics, a great part of its success is due. As the years went by, he constantly enlarged and broadened the scope of his operations. He was among the first outside the very large cities to departmentalize a dry goods store, and among the first to take advantage of collective buying, identifying himself with a New York syndicate whose yearly purchases amount to over $200,000,000. His gift of leadership led him early in his career to surround himself with men of ability and business capacity, and his organization today is strong and capable. Realizing that the best men are not found but made, Mr. Munger has never gone outside of his own organization for a man to manage a department or take a higher position. A strict disciplinarian with those in his training, he would never except less than the best in service, but every buyer and executive in the store in common interest, a whole-hearted neighborly feeling of good will towards an institution which is the convivence and pride of those it serves, and an institution which by sheer worth has won for itself a most enviable position and reputation.

Making the proverbial start in 1869 in the Fox Block in Herkimer, Henry G. Munger founded an enterprise that he has seen forced to move six times in order to accommodate the growth and expansion of the business. In 1869, Mr. Munger had one clerk, and it was his custom to open the store himself in the morning and to lock it at night. He bought practically all the goods that came into the store and sold a large percentage of them. In addition to this, he was his own bookkeeper and general manager. The success of today was not obtained without effort but required years of study and toil. The first move from the modest store of 1300 square feet in the Fox Block to the larger quarters in the Herkimer National Bank building seemed a momentous event. Some years later, he today is ready to give eager testimony as to the beneficial results.

Mr. Munger was the first man in Herkimer to employ a woman clerk, and today, the store employes over 100 women and girls. Fifty years of business necessarily causes many changes in personnel, but six members of the store's present force have been identified with it from 30 to 40 years. 10 have been on the store force for over 29 years, and 14 have records of service ranging from 5 to 20 years. With such an organization, it is small wonder that the store is noted for that stability which comes only from collective effort.

Preparations for the golden anniversary reception have been going on for months and involved not only a huge amount of labor but very large expenditures. The interior of the store was decorated with mammoth shields of blue and gold armor and gold leaves; roses and ivy were used in abondance. On the second floor, a stage had been erected, and here were shown living models of authentic styles as worn in different periods from 1869 to 1919, many of the costumes worn having been purchased at the Munger's store thirty, forty-nine and fifty years ago. Perry's full orchestra furnished the music for the occasion, being stationed at the mezzanine door. In the basement department, an ivory-colored booth covered with gold roses had been erected and here punch was served to the store's guests. Many stores and mercantile establishments in New York and other large cities and towns in the state sent personal representatives to offer good wishes and greetings, and the store's patrons from Herkimer and the surrounding towns included many of the old friends and patrons as well as a younger generation who will form the future clientele of Munger's.

Not only the people from Herkimer but the surrounding cities and villages of the Mohawk Valley were in Herkimer Friday night to do honor and pay their respects to Herkimer's veteran merchant and most successful businessman, Henry G. Munger, on his completion of fifty active years in the dry good business in Herkimer. The decorations in the store were superb, including 150 gold and blue shields with the figures "50" in gold on a blue background on every pilar in the store. These were most attractive and were enclosed in gold leaves.

The clerks wore badges of different colors, designating the number of years of service. Heading the list, of course, was Mr. Munger with a golden bade with the words "1869, H. G. Munger, Founder, 1919." The royal purple was worn by fire whose period of service extended from 30 to 40 years.

They were entitled to wear a royal blue badge showing service from 20 to 30 years. And fifteen were red, showing from 10 to 20 years' service. Fourteen were white for 5 to 10 years of service, and 87 wore American Beauty Roses, their period of service being less than five years.

The remembrances include 50 golden roses sent by Mrs. H. G. Munger, in the loving cup presented to Mr. Munger last year at the formal opening of the big store. A sheaf of American Beauty Roses *from the store employees and floral gifts from practically every larger eastern city. A great many of these were concerns with whom Mr. Munger had done business from 40 to 50 years.*

Congratulatory telegrams and letters were received from personal friends, financial institutions and business concerns, showing the wide scope of Mr. Munger's many business interests.

One of the most prominent features of Friday night's reception was that so many of the participants were old friends, and a large percentage were customers of this store for the past 40 to 50 years. The grandsons and granddaughter as well as the grandfathers and grandmothers were all represented.

A pleasing feature was the return to the store of former employees of long ago to pay their respect to Mr. Munger.

The crowd, which numbered 5000, were greatly entertained by the exhibition of old-time customs for home use, street wear and for social events which were staged in the carpet room under the direction of Miss Schermer.

The most popular number was the showing of an old-time wedding, the bride appearing in a wedding gown of 67 years ago, and her attendant, maids, and flower girls were gowned in keeping with that period. This event so appealed to the public's fancy that it was necessary to show it three times.

Antiques were shown throughout the store, and many of them were rare and valuable indeed, including a paisley shawl—a rare beauty. A camel's hair shawl valued at $800 was brought from Europe by Captain Wotten, father-in-law of Delong, the Artic explorer. A shell comb that belonged to the daughter of the first Sachem of Tammany Hall, who was said to be the handsomest man in New York City. Also numerous other articles exemplifying the old-time hand embroidery of the dainty garment of long ago.

The decorations in the front windows of old ivory and gold were of a degree of excellence, which will not be found outside of cities of a half million or over.

All in all it was a great night for old Herkimer and an unheard testimonial to the character, integrity, and business ability of Herkimer's Merchant Prince, Henry Gillette Munger.

H·G·MUNGER&CO'S GOLDEN ANNIVERSARY
HERKIMER, N.Y.
1869 — 1919

WE EXTEND A CORDIAL INVITATION TO ATTEND OUR

FIFTIETH ANNIVERSARY CELEBRATION
Friday Eve., June 6, 1919—Reception at 7:30

AMONG THE MANY ENTERTAINMENT FEATURES ARRANGED FOR FRIDAY EVENING WILL BE A CONCERT ON THE MEZZANINE FLOOR BY PERRY'S FULL ORCHESTRA, ANIMATED MODELS ON THE SECOND FLOOR SHOWING COSTUMES FROM 1869 TO 1919, PUNCH AND WAFERS IN THE BASEMENT DEPARTMENT; ANTIQUES SHOWN THROUGHOUT THE STORE.

OUR GREAT GOLDEN ANNIVERSARY SALE, JUNE 7th TO JUNE 16th

FIFTY YEARS AGO—AND NOW

MEMORY halts on the hilltop marked by the fiftieth milestone, and looks back across the years to the little store established in the Fox Block on Herkimer's main street in 1869. With but 1300 feet of space, kerosene lamps, and a force of three clerks, the parent store gave little promise of the great enterprise which has resulted from it.

A firm or an individual starts a business in a modest way, with no thought of the magnitude to which it may grow, but interested only in putting into it the very best effort possible. The day-by-day performance of duties, pleasant and otherwise, but always performed with the interest, enthusiasm and energy necessary to the success of any work, results after a few years in a fair measure of success. Memory looks back with pleasure on the attainments of this business at ten years of age. Twenty years brought a greater measure of success, and thirty years brought added success and a growing sense of the expansion possibilities of a department store. Forty years saw many of these expansion possibilities realized, saw the store established in commodious quarters in the Earl and Masonic Blocks, and conducting business on the approval plan of the modern department store.

Situated in the heart of a rapidly growing community, and with transportation facilities giving free access to the store from all directions, it was enabled to cater to a clientele of 75,000 people in this and surrounding territory, and it seemed the store, on its forty-eighth birthday had reached the zenith of its success.

BUT in February, 1917, fire proved the agency selected to test our metal, and with everything gone but our organization, we were required either to retire from the business field or to prove our faith in our own ability by going on.

After forty-eight years of business life and success there are many arguments in favor of terminating a business career, but forty-eight years of service leave their mark, and the plea of our public that we continue to serve could not go unheeded.

So a new store arose, a store endowed with the institutional prestige of the forty-eight years of successful existence of its predecessor, a store with a character and a personality which are the product of years of successful store-keeping, and which are equally as important to the success of the present establishment as the highly specialized methods of store operation, and mechanical equipment for which Munger's is famous.

It is a far cry from the store of 1869 to the one of to-day, but there is a golden link between. Old customers once more in memory visit the old store. There enter again representatives of the town's best-known families, and of families from the surrounding districts, to seek the comforts and necessities of daily living. Some of the old friends and patrons remain. Others have given place to the sons or grandsons, daughters or granddaughters, or to new families altogether, for our community has changed in many respects.

SERVICE gained, and service has retained, these business friendships. The keynote of our success has been service, and we can think of no more fitting way of celebrating the Fiftieth Anniversary of the founding of this business, and of showing our appreciation of the steadfast support of our purchasing public than by rendering on a larger scale than ever before a merchandising service, coupled with phenomenally low prices, which will find expression in a

MAMMOTH GOLDEN ANNIVERSARY SALE

The New York Office of
H. G. Munger & Co.

In the early days the proprietor of H. G. MUNGER'S STORE not only kept his own books and attended to all correspondence, but also he was directly responsible for every dollar's worth of merchandise that entered the store. He bought it all—and unquestionably he bought it well.

To-day, however, a staff of highly specialized buyers and a separate New York office organization are required to keep this splendid institution in the forefront of progress and public favor. Though much of the success and prestige of a retail store depends upon the personality and judgment of its own buyers, the advantages derived from our New York office are so distinctly unusual that perhaps a few words regarding its machinery and capabilities will be of interest to readers who depend upon Munger's for correct fashions and top values.

In the throbbing heart of America's commercial life and linked with one hundred and twenty-five of the largest and finest retail establishments throughout the United States, the New York office of H. G. Munger & Co. represents a co-operative buying force of more than $200,000,000 a year.

The advantages are obvious: In addition to the usual discounts granted by manufacturers to individual stores, extra allowances of substantial size are frequently procured by virtue of the enormous collective purchases placed through this agency and later distributed to all stores participating. Fifty expert buyers scour the markets daily, and as all merchandise is purchased directly from manufacturers, the expensive middleman is entirely eliminated.

The Anniversary Celebration

BEGINNING FRIDAY EVENING, JUNE 6th, AND CONTINUING UNTIL MONDAY, JUNE 16th.

will be for our customers the Golden Harvest of our Golden Year—the greatest year of the half century of this store, and the most important event of the year! We have been telling you that this was the time for celebrating our Golden Year, and that many days would be marked by special features of advantage to our customers. This program will be carried out to the letter. Many thousands of dollars which might figure in legitimate profits will be distributed among our patrons through the great Fifty Year Anniversary Week with the

GREAT GOLDEN ANNIVERSARY SALE OPENING SATURDAY MORNING, JUNE 7th.

We are Distributing This Week a FOUR PAGE CIRCULAR Containing Hundreds of Golden Anniversary Bargains

If you do not receive a copy write us and we will send you one.

Every Dept. Manager

has definite orders to provide a diversified assortment and large quantities, at prices materially below the market value. When such merchandise can be procured in the manufacturing market at a substantial concession in price—and scores of manufacturers have made such concessions—we, as well as our customers, share the benefit. But in numerous instances we shall have to curtail profits in order to insure the necessary variety and the necessary reduction in price to make this GOLDEN ANNIVERSARY SALE ONE THAT WILL GO DOWN IN HISTORY.

OUR PERSONAL SERVICE RECORD.

Is a cause for just pride. Our founder, Mr. H. G. Munger, has been the motive power of this business for fifty years. Six members of the present force have been identified with the business thirty to forty years, ten have been here over twenty years, and thirty-six have been here over five years. It is a record which speaks of the reliability, the experience and the stability of our permanent force, and one which reflects honor upon these co-workers, and the organization of which they are a vital part.

Watch for Our 4-page Circular Containing items in our Anniversary Sale

REMEMBER—OUR GREAT
GOLDEN ANNIVERSARY SALE
Commences Saturday Morning, June 7th, '19

Hundreds of the most attractive bargains the Mohawk Valley has ever known. A fitting way to celebrate our 50 years in business with special prices for those who have helped us to succeed.

Richfield Springs Mercury
June 5, 1919
[Resized from Original]

H·G·MUNGER & CO'S
GOLDEN ANNIVERSARY

1869 · 1919

WE EXTEND A CORDIAL INVITATION TO ATTEND OUR

FIFTIETH
Anniversary Celebration
FRIDAY EVENING, JUNE 6th, 1919
RECEPTION AT 7:30

Our Great Golden Anniversary Sale June 7th to June 16th

FIFTY YEARS AGO!

The Anniversary Celebration

Mammoth Golden Anniversary Sale

MAIN FLOOR IN OUR NEW STORE

Every Department Manager

THE NEW YORK OFFICE OF H. G. MUNGER & CO.

WATCH FOR OUR 4-PAGE CIRCULAR WHICH IS DISTRIBUTED THIS WEEK

H. G. Munger & Company's
Golden Anniversary
June 7th to June 16th
Herkimer Citizen – June 3, 1919
Full page advertisement
[Resized from Original]
From the files of the
Herkimer County Historical Society
Herkimer, Herkimer Co., NY

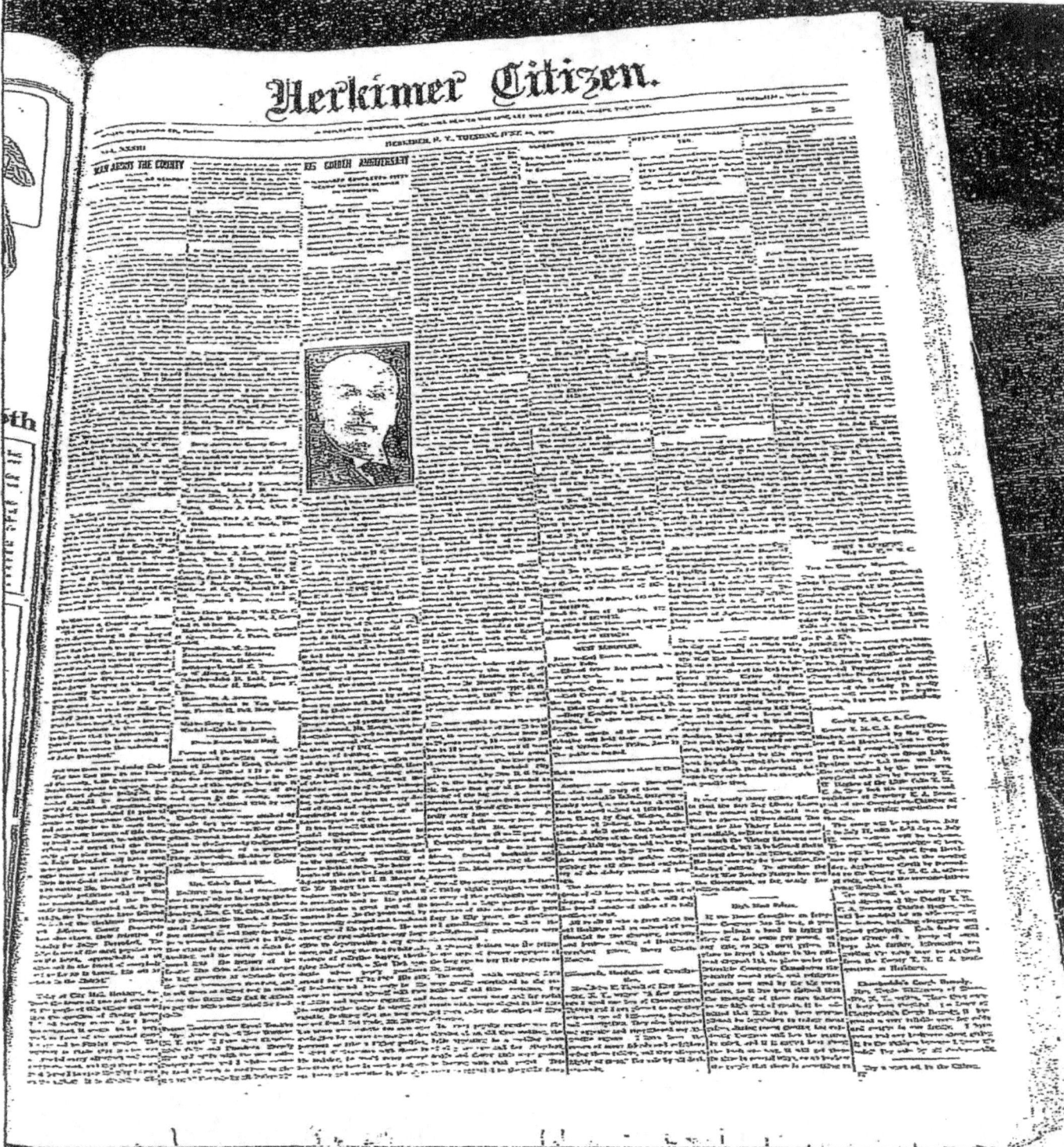

Front Page of the
Herkimer Citizen – June 10, 1919
Herkimer, New York
Article on H. G. Munger & Co.'s
Golden Anniversary
From the files of the Herkimer Co. Historical Society

Music Saturday
from 2:00 to
5:00 by Perry's
Orchestra

H. G. Munger & Co.'s Values Are Always Best

6-14-19

H. G. Munger & Co.

HERKIMER, NEW YORK

Shop in
the morning
if
Possible

Only Two More Days in Our Great
Golden Anniversary Sale

THE GREATEST SALE THE MOHAWK VALLEY HAS EVER KNOWN

The purchases count in thousands daily. There is nothing phenomenal about the outcome of our great planning The goods are here—they are needed merchandise—the prices are indisputably the greatest reduction prices ever placed on merchandise in the valley. There are not merely so-called "leaders" in each department, but each section of the store is contributing scores of bargain items. If we did not have even two more sale days to go, the sale is a tremendous success. Thousands of people thruout the valley have been benefited. Two of the best plans of advertising are: Perfect honesty and in putting out to the public the goods you have for sale, and getting the people into the store to see for themselves.

The honesty of H. G. Munger & Co.'s advertising is never disputed. Thousands of people have seen the bargains and stocked up for summer, and thousands of the people have come because they were told by friends and neighbors of the magnitude of our Golden Jubilee offerings.

Those of you who have been told about this sale, those of you who have read about it, and those who have not yet had an opportunity to attend, let us say to you: "Your opportunities are nearly as great today for money saving as any day during the life of the sale, and your advantages will be waiting for you up until the bell rings at 6 Monday night." REMEMBER —THIS SALE CLOSES MONDAY, JUNE 16th.

Advertisement Dated June 14, 1919
From the Files of the Herkimer County Historical Society
[Resized from Original]

Silks, Dress Goods, Linens and Wash Goods — North Aisle, Rear, Main Floor

Notions, Jewelry and Toilet Goods Section — Center Aisle, Main Floor

Frankfort Citizen newspaper, Frankfort, NY
June 6, 1919
Photo's
Advertising Munger's Golden Anniversary
[Resized from Original]
[Posted on Herkimer County Historical Society's Facebook page.]

Continued on next page.

BASEMENT DEPARTMENT

Cut Glass Section — Basement Department

CHAPTER NINE
MUNGER'S DURING THE ROARING TWENTIES
[The American Department Stores Co. Buys H. G. Munger & Co.]

On **March 28, 1921**, **Henry Gillette Munger** celebrated his **seventy-fifth birthday**.

The **Richfield Springs Mercury, April 7, 1921**, reported, *Seventy-five Years Young* – *H. G. Munger, the veteran department store manager of Herkimer attained his 75-birthday anniversary Monday, March 28th. He was showered with thousands of congratulations by friends in Central New York, where he has become so well-known through the great business he has built up to more than fifty years of intelligent and persistent effort.*

When the big store was destroyed by fire a few years ago, it was frequently remarked that Mr. Munger deserved a rest from the activities of business and many believed he would not rebuild his store and continue in trade. But with renewed energy and determination, he took hold of the big job and in a few months erected one of the finest stores in the state and filled it with an endless variety of staple goods, and already is doing a bigger business than ever before.

In **July** of **1921**, **H. G. Munger & Co**. took Broadway by storm.

An old unidentifiable newspaper clipping dated **July 20, 1921**, reported, *Important New York Contract Awarded H. G. Munger & Co.* – *The largest out-of-town contract ever handled by a Herkimer store has recently been awarded to H. G. Munger & Co. This contract calls for the entire furniture for a new theater recently erected by the Sanjor Theater Corporation, West Forty-First St, New York City, which is the busiest section of any large city in the world.*

The interior of this modern playhouse is carried out in early renaissance and is probably the most beautiful of New York's many famous theaters. The ceiling is most elaborately timbered and a plastic ornament relief in Circassian walnut effect is used throughout the entire house, this being relieved by gold leaf.

The house (theater) is to be carpeted throughout with Wilton velvet in taupe. This includes the main auditorium, all foyers, balconies and boxes. Over 2000 yards of Wilton will be required for the contract, all of which must be laid on concrete and marble, necessitating the drilling of some 33,000 holes for sockets, which in itself is no small task.

One of the unusual features of the theater is the effect obtained at the proscenium arch. This lofty arch is draped with a wide valance of velour and side draperies which remain stationary when the act curtain is raised.

The act curtain is also of velour and hangs directly back of the valence and over-drapery.

All boxes and exits are draped with velour the same as used at the proscenium arch and trimmed with metal gallon in various widths, metal fringes and heavy bullion tassets. The velour used in mulberry tone with grey tracery, used in conjunction with gold silk damask and complementary bullion trimmings.

The workrooms of the local store are busily engaged on this contract and A. P. Jackson returned this morning from New York, where another force of men is employed. Much interest has been shown in the work, which is going forward, and a small window display has been arranged showing some of the fabrics and trimmings used, in order that friends of the store may see them before shipment. Lack of space, of course, makes it impossible to make any adequate display of this work.

During the past ten years or more, our local store has been going farther afield each year in contract work of this kind, and the competition is keen. Their efforts have been uniformly successful. That success attracts "successful" is proved by the fact that this contract was awarded to H. G. Munger & Company, who entered the lists in competition with many other concerns, all proven ability.

Author's Notes:
My research indicates that the above theater in question is the "**National Theater**," located at **208 W. 41st Street** in **NYC**, then owned by the **Sanjor Theater Corporation**. The 1, 235 seat theater opened on **September 1, 1921**, with the opera "**Swords**" starring American operatic soprano and impresario **Emma Abbott**. The **National Theater** was the only new theater, in NYC, to have opened in **1921**, financed by theater agent **Walter C. Jordan** and designed by **William Neil Smith**.

In **1927**, the **Shubert** brothers purchased the theater. Theater impresario **Billy Rose** purchased the theater in **1959**, renaming it after himself, "**Billy Rose Theater**."

In **1978**, the **Nederlander Organization** purchased and refurbished the theater renaming it the "**Trafalgar Theater**." Two years later, in **1980**, the theater was once again renamed: This time in honor of **David T. Nederlander**. The **Nederlander Theater** in NYC is still in operation today, as of this writing.

———————

The **Otsego Farmer** newspaper, **September 23, 1921**, reported, *three shoplifters operated within the last few days at the store of H. G. Munger & Co. of Herkimer and got away with dresses valued at around $200. Two of the party visited the cloak and suit department and the younger of the two was the prospective purchaser while the older one did the talking, and many suits and* *dresses were inspected during the visit. The older woman was relieved by a third party and after all had left, it was disclosed that three dresses were missing.*

In late **November 1922**, H. G. Munger once again expanded his department store with the purchase of the three-story "**Grogan Block**," from T. M. Grogan's widow. This block, directly to the right of Munger's new building, once housed the **Grand Opera House** on its top floor. The entrance to the opera house was through an entrance on the far-right side façade of the building and up the stairs.

An article in the **Richfield Springs Mercury, November 30, 1922**, reported in part, *What is generally regarded in Herkimer as the largest and most important real estate transaction of many months took place last week when H. G. Munger purchased the large Grogan Block on North Main Street."*

An article in The **Utica Observer Dispatch, February 3, 1923**, read "**Munger Company Expand Store** - *The department store of H. G. Munger & Co. is to be expanded by including the second floor of the Grogan Block, recently purchased from Mrs. Mary Grogan.*

Plans for remodeling the second floor will give several additional feet of floor space, being estimated at 5,000 square feet, and these will soon be made ready by the architect.

The Briggs Dancing Academy on the third floor will not be affected by the change except that provision for coat and restrooms must be made on the third floor.

The addition to the Munger store will give floor space equal to that of the largest city stores and will increase its trading facilities.

The purchase of the "**Grogan Block**" was the first step toward expansion taken by Mr. Munger since the erection of the modern building, following the fire of **1917**.

The **Utica Observer Dispatch**, dated **September 16, 1923**, reported, *Munger Store Shows Fine Improvements – Herkimer, Sept. 15 – During the past few months, the Grogan Block has been undergoing a complete change. Workmen have been busy erecting a completely new front, and entirely remodeling the second and third floors. Now the work has been completed and today, H. G. Munger & Company has opened a new furniture department.*

The doorway has been cut through the wall of the present store opening on the second floor of the Grogan Building, where there has been arranged this new department, a model in artistic and decorative features, over carpets of deep blue and surrounded by numerous colorful lamps and artistic mirrors.

The furniture is especially well displayed. One of the features which pleased those attending the first day of the opening was a model dining room furnished with a walnut suite.

Incorporated in this new department are storage, finishing and receiving rooms for furniture, and interior decorating and upholstery rooms and a wallpaper storage room.

Fifty-four years ago, when this store first started in business, the total floor space was only 1,800 sq. feet, while today, this department which has just been opened is almost ten times as large as the entire original store.

The new **H. G. Munger & Co**. **Furniture Department** opened on **September 15, 1923**.

Ellen Arville (nee **Searles) Munger, H. G. Munger's** wife, died on **February 19, 1924**, at **Winter Park, Orange Co., Florida.**

An obituary which appeared in the **Richfield Springs Mercury** newspaper, dated **February 28, 1924**, read, *Mrs. H. G. Munger – Mrs. Ellen Searles Munger died on February 19th at Winter Park, Florida where she was visiting with her husband Henry G. Munger, head of the H. G. Munger & Co. store in Herkimer.*

Mrs. Munger was one of the organizers of the Old Ladies' Home in Mohawk, was president of the board for many years and last year was made honorary president. She was a member of the General Nicholas Herkimer Chapter, D. A. R., serving as regent for 11 years. She was also a member of the General Nicholas Herkimer Homestead Association and of the Mayflower Association. She was also very active in the affairs of Christ Episcopal Church.

She was the daughter of Mr. and Mrs. William T. Searles of Belleville, Jefferson County, where she was born Nov. 8, 1847. There she was married on March 18, 1867, moving to Herkimer in 1869. She leaves four daughters, Mrs. Robert E. Steele of Schenectady Mrs. M. H. Johnson, Utica, and Mrs. G. P. Simmons of Herkimer, and one son, Fred S. Munger of Utica.

There are also two brothers, George W. Searles of Herkimer and the Rev. Edward Searles of Michigan and one sister, Mrs. Ida Plumb of Auburn, and there are 11 grandchildren. A daughter, Mill Alice Munger, died about five years ago, and a son, Bruce, died in infancy.

It is understood the remains will be brought forth. In the death of Mrs. Munger, Herkimer loses a woman of beautiful character, who graced and helped every effort for good."

Mrs. Munger was buried at the **Oak Hill Cemetery** in Herkimer, NY.

In **March** of **1925**, H. G. Munger left on a six-week cruise of the **Mediterranean** and a motor tour through **Southern Europe**.

When Mungers arrived home, many of his employees threw him a surprise party, welcoming him back.

The **Utica Observer Dispatch, May 2, 1925**, reported, *Given Surprise – Newport, May 2 – About 90 employees of H. G. Munger & Co. of Herkimer tendered a surprise party to Mr. Munger at "Three Islands," Newport, last night in honor of his return from a several months long trip to Europe.*

A few weeks later, the paper reported on **Munger's** trip abroad in their **May 17, 1925**, edition, with a headline reading, *Veteran Herkimer Merchant Back After Trip Abroad, Report European Conditions Show Vast Improvement.* In part, the article read, *Back from a six weeks' cruise of the Mediterranean and a motor tour through Southern Europe, H. G. Munger, Herkimer's veteran businessman, expressed himself optimistically on conditions in the war-torn countries, pointing to many hopeful signs of readjustment that he observed during the trip, not the least of which was rapidly improving business conditions both in France and Italy.*

In Italy, people are happier and earning more money than ever before," Mr. Munger stated, adding that Premier Mussolini had apparently made his people more contented. Both in France and Italy, he observed, shopkeepers report business as on the upgrade.*

On **February 1, 1928**, the **H. G. Munger & Co.** was sold to the **American Stores Company**, a **Philadelphia** based holding company.

With **American Stores Company's** acquisition of the **H. G. Munger & Co.**, H. G. Munger's grandson, **Henry M. Simmons** (son of H. G.'s daughter **Bertha**), was promoted from the **head of advertising** to **store manager**.

With the acquisition, **H. G. Munger** retired from active management in the firm which he had founded. He, however, was kept on, in an elder statesman **advisory role** until his death in 1933.

The **Cherry Valley Gazette** reported **February 10, 1928,** *H. G. Munger Store at Herkimer Sold to Group Owners – H. G. Munger & Company, one of the largest mercantile institutions in the Mohawk Valley, became associated with the American Department Stores through terms of an agreement Wednesday at New York. F. S. Munger, treasurer of H. G. Munger & Co., declined to make public any approximate estimate of the amount involved.*

The transaction does not affect the real estate or buildings, but only includes the business and assets of the store. Besides making the largest business deal which has taken place in Herkimer during the past decade, it signalized the retirement from active interest of the firm's founder and head, Mr. H. G. Munger, who for over 59 years has successfully directed the destinies of the huge enterprise here.

The store did retain its name "**H. G. Munger & Co.**"; however, there was a change in leadership.

Taking over the management of the store was **H. G. Munger's** grandson, **Henry Munger Simmons**.

Henry Munger Simmons was born in **Utica, NY** on **October 20, 1899**, the son of **G. Philip Simmons** and **Mrs. Bertha** (nee **Munger**) **Simmons**. Bertha was a daughter of **H. G. Munger**.

In **Utica**, Henry attended private schools.

In **1912**, his father, **G. Philip Simmons**, who was in the merchandise brokerage business in Utica, moved his family to Herkimer, NY. Here he accepted the vice presidency of the **Horrocks Desk Co.**

Author's Notes:
It is interesting to note that **H. G. Munger's** brother-in-law, **George Walton Searles**, came to Herkimer in **1894** to help organize the **Horrocks Desk Company** in partnership with **William Horrocks** and **H. G. Munger**.

————————

In Herkimer, **Henry M. Simmons** went to public high school, graduating in three, not four years. He was a member of the graduating class of **1916**.

Next, Henry would attend **Phillips Academy** at **Andover, Massachusetts**, later going to **Yale University**.

However, before completing his studies at Yale, he had made a name for himself in athletics, being one of the **best lightweight wrestlers** turned out by the university.

After leaving Yale, Henry found employment, for a short time, with the **American Express Co.**, in **New York** and **Philadelphia**.

Henry next took a course from the **Amos Parrish Advertising Agency**, hoping to make a career in advertising for himself.

After completing the advertising course, Henry's grandfather, H. G. Munger, offered Henry a job with **H. G. Munger & Co.**, doing advertising work for him. Henry accepted the job.

In **1928**, when the **American Department Stores** purchased the **H. G. Munger's** store, its founder, **H. G. Munger**, retired. American Department Stores saw the potential in H.G.'s grandson, taking **Henry** from the **advertising department** to **manager** of their newly acquired **H. G. Munger**

& Co. store, in Herkimer.

On **August 19, 1929**, **Henry M. Simmons** married **Marjorie Lucy Small**, the daughter of **Edward Small,** the former publisher of the **Herkimer Telegram** and former **Herkimer Postmaster**, and his wife **Nellie** (nee **Parker**) **Small**.

Majorie Lucy Small was born on **March 6, 1902**, in Herkimer, NY. She attended the local school and graduated from **Herkimer High School** in **1919**. Later she attended **Skidmore College** at **Saratoga Springs** and later the **New York School of Fine and Applied Arts.**

The couple, **Henry** and **Marjorie,** had no known children.

In **1933**, following the death of **Henry Gillette Munger**, Simmons was able to purchase back **American Department Stores stock** in Mungers. Simmons then formed the Munger holding company, once more putting the store under local ownership.

Mr. Simmons was elected **president** of the company and **secretary** of the holding company.

Gifts for All the Family

From the Mohawk Valley's Great

CHRISTMAS STORE

A FAIRYLAND of Gifts awaits those who shop at Munger's. Here, at moderate prices, are things of a quality you want to give. Special holiday sales supplement endless Christmas displays. On this page are a few of the many things that the Christmas store is featuring—but a visit here will reveal countless others and prove to be an inspiration in solving the problem of "What to Give."

H. G. Munger & Co.

Herkimer's Christmas Store

The Evening Telegram
Herkimer, NY
December 11, 1924
[Resized from Original]

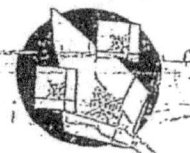

The Cherry Valley Gazette
Cherry Valley, NY
December 9, 1926
[Resized from Original]

H. G. Munger & Co., Announces Anniversary Event

Sixty Years Since H. G. Munger & Co. First Opened

Business Principles of Founder Now Carried On by Large Staff He So Competently Trained in Giving Every Customer Service and Satisfaction

His 60th Anniversary

H. G. MUNGER

Customers Are Invited to Attend Munger's 60th Anniversary Reception
Wednesday Evening, 7 to 9

Manufacturers Send Special Sale Values

Furniture of 1869 In Model Rooms

Historic Wall Papers To Be Described by Authority

Linen Established For Smart Wear

Old Neighbors

Styles of 1869 To Vie With Those of 1929

Historical Booklet Issued For 60th Anniversary

60th Year to Be Celebrated By Herkimer Store

Reception on Wednesday Evening Will Inaugurate Great Store-wide Sale That Marks Sixty Years of Progress for County's Leading Retail Institution

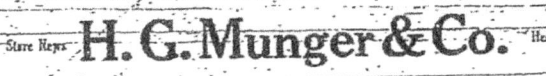

H. G. Munger & Co.

Store Keys — 1869 — 60th Anniversary — 1929 — Herkimer

Use Our Easy CLUB Plan

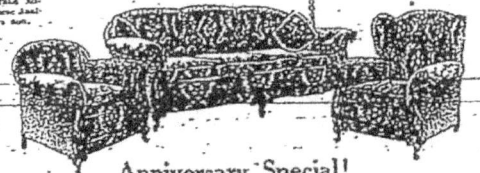

Anniversary Special!
Wagner Living Room Suites
Manufacturer's Co-operation Brings Extraordinary Value

3-pc. Suites Made to Your Order

$160
Ordinarily Sold at $225

Special Anniversary Group!
Dining Room Suites
$216

9-pc. Dining Room Suites of Berkey-and-Gay-and-other Grand-Rapids make. Matched walnut with crotch-mahogany finish. Choice of several styles. Values up to $300.

A Special Purchase!
Fibre Chairs
$9.60

An unusual concession brings this striking sale value. Real stick fibre chairs in assorted colored finishes with loose cushions of bright cretonnes — Regular price $13.25.

Unusual New
Lamps
$5.60

End Table Lamps

Table Lamps, $11.50

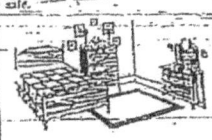

Special Anniversary Group!
Bedroom Suites
$216

4-pc. Bedroom Suites of mahogany and walnut. Berkey and Gay and others in new walnut. Beautiful styles to suit any bedroom. Many of these would sell at $260 to $300.

Anniversary Value!
Cogswell Chairs
$60

Again — Wagner Furniture Co. made possible a splendid anniversary offering. Comfortable Cogswell chairs of regular $89 value — in choice of variety of beautiful colorings.

H. G. Munger and Company
HERKIMER

"Anniversary Offer!
Defiance TUBE FREE

with each Defiance Tire sold during the Anniversary Sale

H. G. Munger & Co
1869 — HERKIMER — 1929

Special Purchase! New Patterns High Grade
Room-Size Wilton Rugs, $60

An extraordinary special! Made possible by manufacturer's co-operation. Beautiful Wilton velvet rugs in sizes 8.3x10.6 and 9x12.

Genuine Gold Seal
Congoleum Rugs

Room-Size
Axminsters

Extra Value
Wall Paper
60c Roll

Exceptional Anniversary Value Group
Quaker Craft Curtains, $2.60

A remarkable anniversary special! A wide selection of designs in filet and shadow net in the popular Egyptian shade.

Gay Patterns in
Cretonnes
60c yd.

Ruffled
Curtains
96c

New Cretonne
Pillows
96c

CHAPTER TEN
MUNGER'S MERGES WITH AMERICAN DEPT. STORES
[Henry Munger Simmons Becomes Munger's New Manager]

As stated previously, On **February 1, 1928**, **H. G. Munger & Co**. sold out to the **American Department Stores Company**, a holding company designed to allow local, privately owned department stores to cut cost by cutting out all the commissions and charges of intermediaries, when purchasing products and goods for their store.

In purchasing these stores, American Department Stores now owned the goods and wares of the store minus the fixtures and building itself and had control over who managed the store and other operational decisions.

Through the merging together of the many stores under their ownership, the American Department Stores Co. had immense buying power in the marketplace.

The **Evening Telegram, Herkimer, NY, February 1, 1928**, reported in part, *H. G. Munger & Company Merged with American Department Stores Today – Approximately Million Involved and Founder H. G. Munger Retires – Backed by American Dry Goods Co. – Realty Not Involved – Henry Simmons to be the Manager – H. G. Munger & Company, one of the largest mercantile institutes in the Mohawk Valley, associated with the American Supermarket Stores, through terms in agreement reached today in New York. While the amount involved was not made public, it is said to be approximately a million dollars.*

The transaction does not affect the real estate of the building, but only the assets of the store.

Both sides marking the biggest real estate deal which has taken place in Herkimer during the past decade, signaling the retirement of the firm's founding head, Mr. H. G. Munger, who for over 59 years has successfully operated the huge enterprise here.

Though rumors of the change have been circulating for several days, H. G. and his son F. S. Munger closed the deal in New York yesterday.

They flew Monday night to New York City to meet with L. L. Jay, the chairman of the American Department Store and president of American Dry Goods Company.

The American Dry Goods Company, representing a combined purchasing power of

$200,000,000, is an outgrowth of the American Department Stores, an operating group directed by Mr. Jay, who has been a business and personal friend of Mr. H. G. Munger.

Simmons New Manager:

By appointing a manager to direct the store, the new firm will not disturb the present organization. Henry Munger Simmons, grandson of H. R. Munger, and son of Mr. and Mrs. G. P. Simmons of this village, will take charge of the store.

Mr. Simmons for the past six years has been the advertising manager for the store, and a graduate of Yale University and is a man whose merchandising skills have steadily increased the sales volume since his connection with the store.

Simmons said today that the store's operation will be identical to the past. "In fact, Mr. H. G. Munger will continue to have an office in the building for his private business affairs and will be retained, by American Dry Goods, in an advisory way," said executives of the new organization.

None of the employees, numbering over 100, or the 18 original executives will be affected by this change, Simmons said, but brought in closer touch to a business they have helped grow. It was this thought, as to the future welfare of his associates, Mr. Simmons said, which have influenced Mr. Munger in his 82nd year, to make the following announcement concerning the store and regarding plans.

Plans For the Future:

To those who have watched the growth of H. G. Munger & Co., this announcement is not a surprise. It is, indeed, a logical step to a greater future.

"No change will be made in the personnel of the store. The salespeople, many of whom you know, will continue to give the same pleasing and courteous service.

"Buyers, who for years have studied preferences and needs of the residents of this Mohawk Valley, will continue to procure the choicest values of the market.

"The management will continue in the hands of those who have grown up with the business. Trained in the art of pleasing and efficient service, these executives will be given even greater authority to carry out the ideals of this institution.

"Mr. H. G. Munger, whose efforts alone, through the fifty-nine years, has built the store to its present enviable position, will continue as a guide and counsellor to those whom he has trained.

"The liberal policies of adjustments and guarantees which assure you of the finest merchandise

remains unchanged. No fairer or more satisfactory policy can be devised.

"The goods themselves which have won the approval of our customers will continue to be procured from the same sources. These are the most reliable that the market affords.

"Prices will, in all probability, be somewhat lower. A vast combined purchasing power of nearly $200,000,000 will bring real savings to everyone.

"Newest methods of inventory stockkeeping, of price levels and of records have been installed. These added advantages combined with saving affected in our great buying organization predict a future that can only be rivaled by the record of past history.

During his business career, Mr. Munger took many of those who had helped to develop the enterprise into the firm with him. Many of them, some since passed away, were present for the golden anniversary. Six had been identified with the business for over thirty years; ten for over 20 years; and thirty-six for over five years.

Despite his age, Mr. Munger has always maintained firm control of the enterprise, although in recent years his son, F. S. Munger, has handled some of the purely business details. Mr. Munger, however, has always been a merchant and his grasp of the retail system built up in the store will be relinquished from strong hand. Hundreds of associates in the town and many friends who respect the judgement and starling qualities of this merchant, while regretting his retirement from active business life, will be glad to know his interest in the store he founded and guided to success will be continued in an advisory capacity.

To his grandson, Mr. Simmons, who will take over the reins under the new management, friends of the store will wish him every success; wishes backed by confidence in the record he has already established with the organization.

E. L. Jackson, who has been associated with the company for many years and is now its vice president, will continue with the change in the business. Other veterans in the store will also continue their connection so that while Mr. Munger will no longer be at the head, the organization he built up will carry on the principles and ideals of the business.

Author's Notes:
According to **H. G. Munger's obituary** (1933), in **February of 1928**, H. G. Munger resigned as president from the company which he had founded when **H. G. Munger & Co.** was sold to the **American Stores**. With American Stores Company's acquisition of the H. G. Munger & Co., H. G. Munger's grandson, Henry M. Simmons (son of H. G.'s daughter Bertha), was promoted from the head of advertising to store manager. That spring when ownership of the Munger's company returned locally, H. G. Munger, age 87, was reinstated as the company's president, retaining his grandson, Henry M. Simmons, as acting manager of the Munger's store.

Henry M. Simmon's obituary (1938) states that *Five years ago (1933) after death of H. G. Munger, his (H. G.'s) interest was bought back and Munger holding company formed, once more putting the store under local ownership. Mr. Simmons was elected president of the company and secretary of the holding company.*

We do know, by the above article, that when American Department Store took over Munger's, they retained H. G. Munger in an advisory role.

––––––––––

CHAPTER ELEVEN
THE DEATH OF HENRY GILLETTE MUNGER
[March 28, 1846 – July 14, 1933]

The headline of **The Evening Telegram**, Herkimer, NY, **July 14, 1933**, read, *Dean of Businessmen And Community Leader Passes Quietly At Home – Beloved Merchant Prince Who Built Small Store Into Mighty Mercantile Business in 63 Years While Founding Banks and Industry as Well as Making Political History Goes to Beyond at Age of 87.*

In part, this is how his obituary read: *Henry Gillette Munger, 87, pioneer Merchant, manufacturer, banker and onetime county political leader, passed away quietly last night at his North Main Street home. The man who probably had more to do with the development of Herkimer in the past 70 years than any other died after lingering in a critical condition for three days, suffering from pneumonia. He had been sinking rapidly for the past two weeks and his health had failed steadily for the past two years.*

The end came at 9:10 p.m.

Death came with his daughters, Mrs. M. H. Johnson, Cambridge, Massachusetts, Mrs. G. R. Jewett, White Plains, and Mrs. G. P. Simmons at his bedside, in addition to other relatives.

Until his last illness, Mr. Munger retained his mental faculties and could recall vividly minor events in his life dating back more than half a century. Of later years, a dignified pleasant white-haired man, he continued to find as much pleasure in meeting people as in the days when he helped mold village history. At the time of his death, he was chairman of the board of the First National Bank and a titular head of the H. G. Munger and Co. store which he founded 63 years ago.

He resigned in Feb. 1928, when it was sold to chain interests, but that spring when ownership of the store returned locally, he again accepted the presidency at the age of 87.

From those first years as proprietor of a 17X19 store, he took an active part in almost every sort of community activity. Reviewing his many interests, it is difficult to understand how he found time for all of them.

Realizing the value of advertising, he combined it with shrewd merchandising to make the Munger store one of the greatest of its time in the Mohawk Valley. In so doing, he performed a valuable service for his community by making it a trading center and bringing development that would not otherwise have been possible.

Possessing faith not only in his own interpretation of the community's desires but also in the future of the community in which he had labored half a century, Mr. Munger was put to an extreme test in 1917 at the age of 70, when fire in an hour wiped out the material evidence of all his labors. In less than a year, a larger, more beautiful store was opened to the public.

Politics His Hobby

If Mr. Munger could be said to have possessed time for a "hobby" in a lifetime crammed with accomplishment, it was politics. Recalling his 46 years' connection with Mr. Munger, E. L. Jackson, as vice president of his department store, today declared Mr. Munger received more pleasure from this diversion than almost anything else.

Because his reign in politics was many years ago, few of the present generation realize the power he wielded.

An ardent Republican, he became county chairman and served as delegate in 1892 to the convention, which renominated President Benjamin Harrison and in later years that which nominated Calvin Coolidge.

Mr. Munger nurtured the late Warner Miller in politics and almost single-handedly negotiated his election as United States senator. His encounters with Titus Sheard are [not readable] of political history in the county.

He was often urged to run for office but never consented, believing that his manifold interest in business and community affairs did not give him time.

Banking also attracted Mr. Munger early in his business career. In 1884, together with Henry Churchill and Palmer M. Wood, he organized the First National Bank of this village. He served as its president for many years. Last year, when the bank consolidated with the Herkimer National Bank, he was elected chairman of the board.

He was one of the organizers and for many years served as president of the First National Bank in Frankfort, resigning in 1925.

Organized Horrocks Desk Co.

A third major activity in Mr. Munger's life was manufacturing. He founded the Horrocks Desk Company in 1895 together with Henry Horrocks. The deal was closed at an all-night session in Fort Plain. Mr. Munger's son, Frederick B. Munger, became the active guiding hand in the business, which expanded to one of the most important manufacturing plants in the village for many years *and gained a national reputation for its quality output. The son's death in 1920 [sic: 1930] was one of the most severe blows suffered by Mr. Munger, whose faith in his son's business ability and their unusually strong affection was apparent. Mr. Munger retained his connection with the plant a year after his son's death and then resigned.*

While finding time to take part in so many varied activities, Mr. Munger also gave much of his business acumen to his church. He was vestryman for many years of Christ Episcopal Church of which he was a member for more than 60 years. He served on the building committee and had an active part in constructing the present church edifice in 1888.

He attended the 100th anniversary ceremonies a few months ago and was the oldest living member present.

Mr. Munger was, likewise, interested in education and served on the local Board of Education in the '70s. It was during his tenure of office that the first modern school, the former North School, was constructed on Washington Street. Previously on the same site had stood an old district school building. He was a firm believer in doing everything to give the children the best education possible.

Mr. Munger was at one time vice president of the McMillan Book Company of Syracuse.

Many Other Activities

A past president of the board of trustees of Pine Crest Sanatorium Association, he had served continuously by appointment of the Board of Supervisors as a member of the board since the sanatorium was established.

His community activities also included an active part in the development of the Chamber of Commerce, and he was a trustee of Herkimer Free Library for several years. He was a member of the Down and Out Club; Republican Club of New York; Fort Schuyler Club of Utica; and the Mohawk Valley Country Club.

During the World War, Mr. Munger was patriotically interested in the distribution of Liberty Loan bonds and other local movements for the success of the conflict.

Not only was Mr. Munger the first local merchant to departmentalize his store, but he also was the first to employ women clerks. His interest in merchandising was personal and he always made it a point to know personally as many of his customers as possible. His remarkable memory for faces served him well in business.

A few months ago, when Mr. Munger was visiting his store, a woman tapped his arm and said.

"Mr. Munger, I have traded with you a good many years, do you remember me?" Mr. Munger, then 86, looked at her, smiled and said: *"Yes, you are Mrs.____of Ilion. I sold you a plush coat for $45 more than 40 years ago." "That's right,"* said the woman, *"and I still have the coat."*

Loved By Employees

The respect, affection and veneration employees always held for Mr. Munger dates to 1869, when he first started in business here as a member of the firm of Avery and Munger in a small store in what was the Fox Block on North Main Street. Five years later, Mr. Munger took over sole interest and his business started to grow rapidly.

He moved to the Earl Block, now the site of the First National Bank and Liberty Theater, but shortly found more quarters needed and expanded into the adjacent Masonic Block where the store served a constantly growing valley trade until destroyed by fire in February 1917.

The new store, built just south of the ruins, cost Munger $150,000. The Graves Block adjoining the north was added to the store for a time, but even this proved inadequate.

In 1922, the Grogan Block adjoining, one of the largest in the village, was purchased.

He Enjoyed Travel

Before the death of Mrs. Munger, they found time for world travel, which was one of their keen enjoyments. They went abroad several times. Mr. Munger made one trip to Europe after her death with his daughter, Mrs. G. P. Simmons. It was on this journey that he took his first airplane trip from Paris to London.

To Mr. and Mrs. Munger were born six children: a son, Frederick Searles, and five daughters—Mabel Irene, Bertha Ellen, Mary Elizabeth, Frances Lillian and Alice D.—all of whom survive except Alice, Mabel and Frederick. Frederick, treasurer and manager of the Horricks's Co., married Miss Florence Eddy, daughter of Frank Eddy, prominent businessman of Detroit.

To them were born two children: Barbara and Janet. Miss Mable I. Munger married Robert E. Steele, deceased, an attorney and official of the General Electric company until his death. They left two children, Eleanor and Bruce, later connected with the Edison Appliance Co., Chicago. Miss Bartha Munger married George P. Simmons, and their son, Henry M. Simmons, is treasurer and manager of the Munger store. He was graduated from Yale and directed the store during the ownership by the American Department Stores Corp. Elizabeth Munger married G. R. Jewett, New York banker, and they have three children: Elizabeth, Guernsey and Henry. Frances Munger married M. H. Johnson, a retired manufacturer, and they had three sons: Montgomery, Francis and Gregory.

The funeral will be held Saturday afternoon from the late home at 4:30 o'clock with Rev. L. Curtis Denney, rector of Christ Church officiating, assisted by Rev. W. C. Prout of Middleville, former rector here. The burial will be in Oak Hill Cemetery.

In memory of Mr. Munger, the H. G. Munger store will be closed today and Saturday.

All other stores in Herkimer will be closed from 4:30 to 5 o'clock, Saturday afternoon, Burt O. Lee, chairman of the retail merchants announced; and Miss Edith M. Sheaf, Librarian, said that the Herkimer Free Library, of which Mr. Munger was a trustee, will be closed during the same period.

Upon **H. G. Munger's** death, his grandson, **Henry Munger Simmons**, continued to manage the **H. G. Munger & Co**. store.

Author's Notes:
Although **H. G. Munger's** obituary seemed to have covered all bases, there were several **errors** made:

The **first** such error: *Five years later, Mr. Munger took over sole interest and his business started to grow rapidly.*

H. G. Munger severed ties with **C. L. Avery** in **March** of **1872, four years** after opening their store in Herkimer.

The **second** error: *He resigned in **Feb. 1928**, when it was sold to chain interests, but that spring when ownership of the store returned local, he again accepted the presidency at the age of 87.*

It is true that **American Department Stores** did purchase the **H. G. Munger & Co**. in **February** of **1928**, upon which H. G. Munger resigned/retired as the company's **president**. In **Feb. 1928**, H. G. Munger was just shy of his **82**[nd] birthday. It would not be until **March** of **1933**, five months before his death, that he turned **87.**

In truth, **H. G. Munger & Co**. was able to buy back its stock from **American Department Stores** in **1933**, not the **spring of 1928.**

––––––––––––

Late Henry G. Munger's Will Admitted to Probate Today

The will of the late Henry G. Munger, Herkimer business and civic leader, who died July 13, was admitted to probate today by Surrogate Abram Zoller.

The entire estate, as announced recently in the Telegram, goes to relatives of the deceased. Value of the estate was estimated in the petition for proof of the will at personal property of "over $10,000" and real property of "over $10,000," but will greatly exceed this.

The will provides for trust funds for each of his three children surviving him and for the four grandchildren of his two deceased children. Each of the children, Frances M. Johnson, Commercial street, Provincetown, Mass., Elizabeth M. Jewett, 92 Soundview Avenue, White Plains, and Bertha M. Simmons, 665 Renwick avenue, this village, will receive one-fifth of the residuary estate, while each of the four children of Fred S. Munger, and Mabel Munger Steele, will receive a tenth of the residuary estate, or an equal share of the one-fifth left their parents. The grandchildren are Barbara Coonradt, 33 Paris Road, New Hartford, Janet Munger, 766 James street, Syracuse, Eleanor S. Belmer, Chappaqua, and Bruce M. Steele, 1028 Ridgeway, Oak Park, Ill.

Mr. Munger bequeathed $5,000 to each of his three daughters, this amount to be deducted from their share of the estate. He likewise placed a clause in his will to the effect that the amount of money borrowed from him by any of the children during his lifetime be deducted from their share of the estate. An itemized account of such loans accompanied the will.

All of the deceased personal belongings are left to the children, provided they can agree on a division thereof, otherwise they are to be sold and the proceeds of such sale to be distributed "to my issue, per stirpes."

In his will, Mr. Munger provides for annual incomes for each of his children and for his sister, Mary Massee. Each daughter is to receive $1,000 annually for the "corpus" of her trust and his sister is to receive an annual income of $1,500, produced from a trust fund, the amount to be set aside for such trust fund to be determined by the executors and trustees of the will, Guernsey R. Jewett, son-in-law, who resides in White Plains, and Henry J. Munger, nephew, whose home is in South Orange, N. J. The executors and trustees are directed by the terms of the will to advance sums as they find necessary from this trust fund from time to time. Upon the death of Mr. Munger's sister the undistributed part of her trust fund is to be divided equally among Mr. Munger's children.

Another clause in the will provides that when the grandchildren reach the age of 21 the accumulated income from their share of the estate will be paid them and thereafter the entire net income in monthly installments until they reach the age of 40. At the age of 30 both the children and grandchildren of Mr. Munger are to receive one-third of the corpus of each trust; at 35 they are to receive another third and at 40 they will receive the balance.

The will gives the executives and trustees the power to sell securities at such time as they see fit.

One clause reads, "the trustees shall apply the entire income of all securities at any time, forming part of the trust fund to the use of the beneficiary thereof, irrespective of the prices paid for them, or of their market value at any time, it being my intention that no part of such income shall be applied as a sinking fund to offset the gradual loss of the premium upon or the market value of such securities; but my executors in their uncontrolled discretion and obsolence of any other property or assets forming a part of my estate or corpus of any trust without liability on their part, however, in the event of failure to do so."

Mr. Munger authorized the purchase of a monument for his grave at a maximum not to exceed $2,500, and a monument for the grave of his son, Frederick S. Munger, the cost not to exceed $1,000. He also left $100 for the perpetual care of his grave at Oak Hill Cemetery.

CHAPTER TWELVE
THE DEATH OF HENRY MUNGER SIMMONS
[October 20, 1899 – December 16, 1938]

In **February** of **1928**, **Henry Munger Simmons**, a grandson of **H. G. Munger**, who had worked for several years in the advertising department of his grandfather's store, took over the everyday management of the **H. G. Munger & Co**. with the store's acquisition by the **American Department Stores, Co.**

Only months before his death, **H. M. Simmons** had plans drawn up to **modernize** the store which his grandfather had founded.

Then the following happened:
The headline on page one of the **Friday, December 16, 1938**, Evening Telegram, Herkimer, NY read, *H. M. Simmons and Wife Killed When Automobile Rams Truck on Route 5 – President of H. G. Munger Co. and Mrs. Simmons Returning from Little Falls Birthday Party Early Today When Their Machine Plows Into Heavy Vehicle Stalled West of Cemetery in E. Herkimer; Fatality Stuns Village. Removes Two of Most Active and Influential Residents; Dr. Graves Questions Witnesses This Afternoon.*

The paper goes on to report, in part, *Mr. and Mrs. Henry M. Simmons, North Main St., two of Herkimer's best-known citizens, were fatally injured early this morning when their automobile crashed into a parked truck on Route 5 near St. Mary's Cemetery, East Herkimer. The double tragedy left this community stunned and saddened in the midst of its holiday preparations.*

The couple was returning from the home of Mr. and Mrs. Enrique Lopez-Mena, South Ann St., Little Falls, where they had attended a birthday party. Mr. Simmons, whose department store had just started remaining open evenings for the Christmas holiday rush, did not leave his place of business until 9 o'clock. His mother, Mrs. G. P. Simmons, had assisted him in preparing a bag of toys and a Santa Claus costume. He had decided not to dress formally but to go as Santa Claus and surprise his friends. Not even his wife, according to his mother, knew his intention. She had gone to Little Falls earlier in the evening.

Dr. James W. Graves, who investigated the fatalities, said that the truck driver claimed to have placed flares when he stopped on the route to Syracuse. Just what caused the crash may never be known. The impact was terrific, the Simmons sedan telescoping under the rear of the truck with such force as to sheer the right rear wheel from the truck.

Reconstructing the accident from the information available, Dr. Graves said that he believed Mr. Simmons made a desperate effort to swing clear of the truck just before the impact. The left front end of the car was wedged under the truck body at an angle. Marks on the road, he said, indicated that Mr. Simmons had applied his brakes about 50 feet from the truck at a point just past the flare that the truck driver claimed to have been previously set up in the rear.

Mr. Simmons, Dr. Graves believes, died instantly. Mrs. Simmons, although unconscious, probably lived a few minutes.

The truck was driven by George W. Turner, 26, of Syracuse, and owned by Marcella A. Rice of the same city. Turner, sworn by Dr. Graves at the scene of the accident, said he had taken charge of the truck at Albany at 10 p.m. last night. Accompanying him was a helper, George E. Repser, Syracuse.

At a point almost in front of St. Mary's Cemetery, Turner testifies the truck ran out of gas. He said that his first act was to light the red fuses on the rear of the truck. He then set out three flares, he said, one in the rear of the truck, one at the side, and the third in front. The flares were in that position when officials arrived at the scene.

Turner said he hailed a passing truck driver, rode with him to the Clock service station in East Herkimer, obtained some gasoline, and went back to the truck. He poured the gasoline into the tank, he testified, then raised the hood over the motor, and was working the carburetor float up and down, drawing gasoline into the vacuum tank, when he heard the impact. He fixed the time at about 15 minutes after he had first come to a stop.

Joseph Murray, Little Falls, driving eastward saw that an accident had occurred and stopped his car. He told Dr. Graves that he thought Mrs. Simmons was still alive when he opened the right front door of the car. He felt her wrist, he said, but could not detect any perceptible pulse. He then notified Sergeant John W. Brockman of the East Herkimer state police substation who, in turn, notified Coroner Graves. The state police received the call at 1:45 a. m. Dr. Graves arrived at the scene within five minutes of the time he was notified.

Dr. Graves also attempted to ascertain if Mrs. Simmons was still alive but said that he could feel no pulsations. He removed her from the car. It was then found that Mr. Simmons' body could not be removed with the wrecked machine still wedged beneath the truck. Dr. Graves directed Turner to move the truck ahead far enough to clear the car. As Turner did so, the right rear wheel of the truck dropped from the axle.

The back of the front seat had been broken and Mr. Simmons' body was lying partly on the front seat and partly on the rear seat.

In the front seat was the crumpled Santa Claus costume Mr. Simmons had worn earlier in the evening.

Murray told Dr. Graves that he had seen the flares of the truck from a point 500 feet distant from the scene of the crash. Dr. Graves also questioned James DeRosia, Ilion, who was driving west when he passed the scene of the accident. "The first thing I saw as I came over the hill," Dr. Graves quoted DeRosia as testifying, "was the reflection of the red fuse against the sky."

Dr. Graves released Turner on his own recognizance but told him to hold himself subject to call for additional testimony, if necessary. Turner got in touch with his employer who dispatched another truck from Syracuse to remove the merchandise. Mr. Simmons' car was towed to the Patterson garage in East Herkimer. It was almost completely demolished.

There were two prevailing theories as to how the tragic accident happened:

According to the same newspaper article, *Dr. Graves believed that a frost windshield caused by the near-zero temperature may have obscured Mr. Simmons' vision as he neared the parked truck. Numerous drivers reported having had difficulties from frosted windshields during the night. The windshield was so badly shattered, however, that it could not be determined if that condition existed.*

Another theory is that Mr. Simmons may have had difficulty with his brakes. At 9 o'clock last night he drove into the Lanning & Folts garage and reported that one of his rear brakes was frozen. He was going to leave the car there, Mr. Lanning said, but on his advice to try backing the car, the frozen brake loosened. Mr. Simmons then said, according to Mr. Folts, that he would leave immediately for Little Falls in order not to be late.

Norman Briggs, who operates the garage in the rear of the H. G. Munger company store and who has always done the repair work on Mr. Simmons' car, said that he washed the machine yesterday and drove it out into the yard at 6 o'clock last night. He recalled applying the emergency brake, and he believes that it caused the rear wheel brake to freeze later in the evening.

He said that he had also removed the left front tire from the machine yesterday, placing it on the left rear, and placing the one removed from the left rear on the left front. This, he said, would give the car better braking power because the one placed on the rear was more worn, and the extra weight on the front wheels would give the better tread added effectiveness in contact with the ground.

Mr. Briggs said that the car was not equipped with a defrosting device or a fan, such as is used by some drivers to keep the windshield free from ice. The car was equipped with a heater, he said. Mr. Briggs believes that if the windshield had become frosted while Mr. and Mrs. Simmons were in Little Falls, the ice would not have a chance to dissolve or melt away in the short distance the car was driven before the accident. It was his belief that a frosted windshield had caused the tragedy.

Henry Munger Simmons (39) and his wife, Marjorie Lucy (nee Small) Simmons (36), are buried at Oak Hill Cemetery, Herkimer, NY.

This accident left H. G. Munger & Co. without a head. Henry J. Munger, a cousin of Mr. Simmons and an officer in the company, will arrive today from East Orange, NJ. The future policy of the store will probably be decided by its officers shortly.

Author's Notes:
H. J. Munger was, in fact, **Henry Jarius Munger** (1883-1950), a brother of **Henry Gillette Munger**. That would make **H. J. Munger** a **great uncle** of **Henry Munger Simmons**.

––––––––––

The **Utica Daily Press, December 17, 1938**, reported, ***Double Funeral Sunday for Valley Couple Killed in Accident*** – *Funeral services for Mr. and Mrs. Henry M. Simmons, North Main S., victims of an auto-truck accident early Friday morning opposite St. Mary's Cemetery on Route 5, will be held Sunday at 2:30 pm. at Christ Episcopal Church. The Rev. Gordon L. Kidd will officiate.*

In **1937**, a year before his death, **Henry Munger Simmons** was instrumental in obtaining the **Martin & Naylor** department store, located at **45 – 47 North Main St.**, in **Gloversville**, founded in **1890** and one of the largest retail firms in northeastern New York.

Following the death of **Henry Munger Simmons**, longtime Munger's employee **Leon V. Harris** took over as manager of the **H. G. Munger & Co**. department store in Herkimer.

Leon V. Harris was born on **October 29, 1889**, in **Newport, Herkimer Co., NY** to **Myron S.** (1858-1944) and **Mary T.** (nee **Todd**) **Harris** (1861-1917).

On **September 23, 1908**, at Herkimer, NY, **Leon** married **Iva M. Bowen** (1888 – 1972), a daughter of **Theodore Bowen** (1851-1917) and **Emma J.** (nee **Pexton**) **Harris** (1864-1950).

The **Leon** and **Iva** had one known child, **Lura M.** (nee **Harris**) **Bleau** (1911-1997), wife of **William Suters Bleau.**

The **1910 U.S. Federal Census** lists Leon's occupation as a "**Window Trimmer – Dry Goods Store.**"

Leon's **WWI Draft Registration Card**, signed **June 5, 1917**, lists his occupation as "**Advertising Manager – H. G. Munger & Co.**"

The **1920 U.S. Federal Census** lists his occupation as an "**Advertising Manager – Dry Goods Store.**"

"**Assistant Manager & Buyer, Dept. Store**" was Leon's occupation in the **1930 U.S. Federal Census**.

According to an article in the **December 3, 1937**, **The Otsego Farmer**, Cooperstown, NY, *A Christmas bonus of $5393 was distributed to eight-nine employees of the H. G. Munger & Co. department store at Herkimer just after closing Tuesday of last week. Henry M. Simmons, president, made the presentation and issued this statement: "Due to increased business which, of course, meant additional profit, the management of the H. G. Munger & Co. store decided to share that profit with their employees and paid out the equivalent of ten percent of the wages from the period February 1*[st]* to November 1*[st]*."*

H.M. Simmons and Wife Killed When Automobile Rams Truck on Route 5

President of H. G. Munger Co. and Mrs. Simmons Returning From Little Falls Birthday Party Early Today When Their Machine Plows Into Heavy Vehicle Stalled West of Cemetery in E. Herkimer; Fatality Stuns Village, Removes Two of Most Active and Influential Residents; Dr. Graves Questions Witnesses This Afternoon.

**Headline From
Henry Munger Simmons' Obituary
The Evening Telegram**
Herkimer, NY
December 16, 1938
[Resized from Original]

In Double Fatality

HENRY M. SIMMONS

Valley Crash Which Claimed Two Lives

Returning home from a party at Little Falls, Mr. and Mrs. Henry M. Simmons, prominent Herkimer residents, lost their lives in this accident when the Simmons car rammed a parked truck on Route 5, two miles east of Herkimer, early Friday morning.

Double Funeral Sunday For Valley Couple Killed in Accident

Headline From
Henry Munger Simmons' Funeral Article
Utica Daily Press
Utica, NY
December 17, 1938
[Resized from Original]

Henry Munger Simmons, Ph.B. 1920.

Born October 20, 1899, in Utica, N Y.
Died December 16, 1938, in Herkimer, N Y

Father, George Philip Simmons, vice-president Horrocks Desk Company of Herkimer, son of Rev Henry Martin Simmons, D D , and Florence (Head) Simmons of Minneapolis, Minn. Mother, Bertha (Munger) Simmons, daughter of Henry Gillette and Ellen Arvilla (Searles) Munger of Herkimer Yale relatives include an uncle, Frederick S. Munger, '94 S

Foreign exchange trader American Express Company, New York and Philadelphia, 1920–22, associated with H G Munger & Company, a department store in Herkimer, since 1922 (advertising manager 1923–28 and general manager and president 1928–38); director First National Bank of Herkimer (member finance committee), Herkimer Free Library, Herkimer Memorial Hospital, National Retail Dry Goods Association, and American Legion, member Christ Church (Episcopal), Herkimer

Married August 19, 1929, in Herkimer, Marjorie Lucy, daughter of Edward and Nellie (Parker) Small No children

The following write up was found on
Henry Munger Simmons'
Find a Grave Website.

CHAPTER THIRTEEN
MUNGER'S 70ᵀᴴ ANNIVERSARY CELEBRATION
[The Opening of Their Newly Enlarged & Remodeled H. G. Munger & Co. Store]

As stated previously, only months before his untimely death, **Henry Munger Simmons** had plans drawn up to **modernize** the **Munger's** store. However, with his death, it would be **Leon Harris**, Simmons' successor, who was left with this modernization task.

The Evening Telegram, Herkimer, NY, Wednesday, May 17, 1939, featured a full-page advertisement for **Munger's** combined **70th Anniversary Celebration** and its **Modernized Store Opening**.

The advertisement is sectioned off into individual headings and articles in connection with the two celebrations.

One of the headings read, ***Two Couples Representing 1869 and 1939 to Open Doors: Store Closes 4 p. m. Thursday*** – *H. G. Munger & Co. will close the store at 4 p.m. Thursday and reopen at 7 o'clock in the evening for the formal opening and reception celebrating the 70th anniversary of its founding.*

The windows will be veiled, and at 7:15 p. m., two vehicles will arrive at the store bearing "Mr. and Mrs. 1869" and "Mr. and Mrs. 1939." They will open the doors to the public. Both couples will be garbed according to the period and will be carried in coaches corresponding to their times.

Another heading read, ***Munger's Opens New Modern Store on 70th Birthday – Public Reception Thursday Night Inaugurates Event – Dream of H. M. Simmons, Late President, Seen in Modernized Interior, Rearranged Departments, and Addition of Separate Men's Shop in Former Schrott Jewelry Store; Indirect Lighting Installed and Store Redecorated*** – *H. G. Munger & Company, one of the leading department stores in the Mohawk Valley, will celebrate its 70th anniversary with an opening reception for the public in a newly modernized store here Thursday night.*

Planned by Henry M. Simmons, grandson of the founder before his death five months ago, visitors will see many changes in the store during the past weeks.

The main floor has been given a stream-lined effect, the aisles widened, new glass cases and circular counters installed, and a new linoleum floor laid. Indirect lighting around the side walls is broken by shadow boxes for display.

For the store's birthday, honoring H. G. Munger, who established the business in 1869, these hold interesting silhouettes of old stagecoaches, the first trains, the first steamboat, and other historical subjects, the work of Charles Bechtold, display manager.

Many departments have been enlarged, some have been moved to new locations, and all have been improved by new lighted cases.

The shoe shop at the rear has been entirely refurnished with new rugs, chromium chairs and fitting stools.

The sport shop, jewelry shop, closet shop and tiny tot show have also been attractively rearranged and modernized, but one of the most striking improvements, a store officiate said, is the addition of a modern men's shop, located in the annex formed by the addition of the former Schrott's Jewelry Store.

A wide arch connects the men's shop with the main floor, but the annex has its own street entrance for men.

The annex, carrying also a line of luggage, will add a thousand square feet of floor space to the main floor of the store.

Work of improving and modernizing the store was done under the direction of Willard Hulin, local contractor, and Leon Harris, acting manager of the store. Many local carpenters, painters and other workmen have been employed.

Thousands of dollars were spent in the modernization program, but the results, providing customers with a lighter, pleasanter and more convenient place to shop, seemed well worth it, store officials said.

Modern Store Dream of Late H. M. Simmons, read another headline followed by **President of Company, Killed in Motor Crash, Planned Changes Before Death; Succeeded Grandfather During Economic Depression and Brought Store Through Troubled Times –** *The modernized store of H. G. Munger & Co. to be opened Thursday night will be a memorial to Henry M. Simmons, former president killed in an automobile accident with his wife before Christmas, Leon V. Harris, acting manager, said today.*

Mr. Simmons, who was chosen to head the Munger company on the death of his grandfather, H. G. Munger, in 1933, during trying economic times, had laid the plans for expansion and improvement of the store.

Business was suffering from the crash of 1929 which deprived families of their savings, jobs, and their homes when Mr. Simmons took charge of the store. Volume declined, prices dropped, and Mr. Simmons, like other executives, was forced to cut operating expenses, yet maintain the service for which the store was known.

He studied the problem with the thoroughness he applied to every business detail and solved it with consideration for employees and fairness to his organization and to the public.

Through the Depression years, he kept the store's organization intact and continued service to its customers, not without great difficulty.

Those close to him knew he had planned expansion and improvement of the store and was disappointed that exigencies of the times forced postponement of the work. The balance finally turned, and the retail business began to improve.

Mr. Simmons called in experts to study changes to make the store more modern, pleasanter and easier to shop in. With their help, he drew plans for the realization of his dream. In November, a month before his death, they were approved, and work was to begin immediately after Christmas.

In the confusion following his death, the plans were necessarily put aside, but eventually it was decided to proceed with them.

The beautiful, spacious, modern interior of the main floor is the result of his planning and stands as a splendid testament to his ideals of service.

Other headlines in the advertisement were *"**Exhibits Show County History**," "**Store Makes Exhibit of Early Americana**," "**Sales Contest to Mark Munger Birthday Event**," "**Spring Blooms Decorate Store For Anniversary**"* and *"**Pageant Will Mark Opening At Reception**."*

An article in the **Richfield Springs Mercury** newspaper, **May 18, 1939**, read, in part, ***Munger's Gets Portraits of Founder, Grandson*** – *Life-size oil portraits of Henry G. Munger, the founder, and Henry M. Simmons, late president, were unveiled at 4 o'clock this afternoon in Munger's store, inaugurating its 70th anniversary celebration.*

More than 100 employees, ready to leave preparatory to the public opening reception in the enlarged modernized store tonight, witnessed the surprise ceremony on the main floor.

The portrait of Mr. Munger was prepared for the store under direction of his grandson, Mr. Simmons, before his death in December. The portrait of Mrs. Bertha M. Simmons' late son was given by her, daughter of Mr. Munger. Both are the work of the artist Leo S. Trimm of Syracuse.

The paintings are enclosed in wide, old, gold frames which set off the warm colors of the oils.

Both are extremely life-like and beautiful and represent some of the best works of the artist.

Supreme Court Justice Abram Zoller gave a brief memorial address at the unveiling of Mr. Munger's portrait. Read Jewett, grandson of the founder, who is connected with the store, unveiled the portrait.

John W. Calder of Utica, an old family friend, spoke in tribute to Mr. Simmons before his portrait was unveiled by his mother. They were introduced by G. R. Jewett of White Plains, president of H. G. Munger & Company.

The public will have an opportunity to view the portraits when the enlarged and modernized store planned by Mr. Simmons, is formally opened for inspection at 7 o'clock tonight.

They were presented as appropriate recognition of the guidance given by Mr. Munger and Mr. Simmons during their lives to bring the store to its 70th anniversary.

Author's Notes:
As of this writing, the painted portraits of Mr. Munger and his grandson, Henry M. Simmons, are on display at the Herkimer County Historical Society.

———————

An Artist's Sketch
taken from a
full-page article which appeared in the
May 17, 1939, Evening Telegram, Herkimer, NY
of the newly remodeled H. G. Munger & Co. store in downtown Herkimer

Old Store of 1869

Growth of H. G. Munger & Co. in 70 years is illustrated by comparing
the store occupied in 1869 (above) with 1,200 square feet of floor space
and the newly modernized store of 76,000 square feet.

The H. G. Munger & Co.'s first store was first located in the
Fox Block located directly to the right of the old Waverly Hotel
on North Main St., Herkimer, NY
At the time of its opening in May of 1869 the store went by the name
"Avery & Munger"

Munger's Opens New Modern Store on 70th Birthday

PAGEANT WILL MARK OPENING AT RECEPTION

Six Models to Display Costumes of Today and 70 Years Ago in Store Thursday Night.

A colorful pageant depicting costumes worn in the 70 years that will be presented during the closing reception to mark the 70th anniversary of H. C. Munger & Co. Thursday night.

It will be held in the elevated basement on the second floor of the store.

Six models will wear costumes of the period, showing a morning dress, an evening dress, a wedding dress and street and afternoon costumes. Modern garb for the same occasions will be presented in contrast with these Civil War fashions. The costumes are authentic reproductions of fashions of the period and give a glimpse of the lives of those ancestors who, when they planned a dress, carefully chose fabrics that would "wear," for once a dress was made, with its yards of lining, fastening, and boning, it was not lightly cast aside until after long service.

The models wearing the period costumes will be Miss Mary Nagle, Miss Evelyn Griswold, Miss Georgette Barton, Miss Constance Speor, Miss Vivian McClancher, and Mrs. Bertha Flewer.

Two children will also present costumes worn by little tots in the 1860's.

There will be several showings of the costumes beginning at 7:15 p. m. Mrs. Elizabeth Burns, Miss Frances Varney, and Mrs. Anna Hall are in charge of the pageant.

MANUFACTURERS GIVE COOPERATION FOR EVENT

Founded Business in 1869

HENRY C. MUNGER

In a little one-room store, Light, the science of buying merchandise by the feeble glow of kerosene for the retail trade.

MUNGER STORE PROUD OF ITS 'ROLL OF HONOR'

Public Reception Thursday Night Inaugurates Event

Dream of H. M. Simmons, Late President, Seen in Modernized Interior, Rearranged Departments, and Addition of Separate Men's Shop in Former Schrott Jewelry Store; Indirect Lighting Installed and Store Redecorated.

H. C. Munger & Company, one of the leading department stores in the Mohawk Valley, will celebrate its 70th anniversary with an opening reception for the public in a newly modernized store here Thursday night.

Store Makes Exhibit Of Early Americana

Old Store of 1869

Growth of H. C. Munger & Co.

Old Employe Contrasts Store Now and 60 Years Ago

MUNGER'S OPENS NEW BUREAU IN NEW STORE

Two Couples Representing 1869 and 1939 to Open Doors; Store Closes 4 P. M. Thursday

H. C. Munger & Co. will close the store at 4 p. m. Thursday and reopen at 7 o'clock in the evening for the formal opening and reception celebrating the 70th anniversary of its founding.

Sales Contest to Mark Munger Birthday Event

EXHIBITS SHOW COUNTY HISTORY

The first plow made and used in Herkimer county, an ox-bow used when Herkimer was only a cluster of homes, a muzzle-loading gun...

Planned Expansion

MODERN STORE DREAM OF LATE H. M. SIMMONS

President of Company, Killed in Motor Crash, Planned Changes Before Death; Succeeded Grandfather During Financial Depression and Brought Store Through Troubled Times.

CHAPTER FOURTEEN
THE H. G. MUNGER & CO. BRANCHES OUT
(With Stores Opening in Gloversville, NY, in 1937 & Boonville, NY, in 1940)

As mentioned in **Chapter Eleven**, in **1937**, a year before **Henry Munger Simmons** died, **H. G. Munger & Co.** purchased the **Martin & Naylor** department store, located at **45-47 North Main St.**, in **Gloversville, Fulton Co., NY.**

The Gloversville store dated back to **1890**, when partners **John Martin** (1847 – 1917) and **Edwin Charles Naylor** (1860 – 1950) purchased the business of **Dan Edwards & Son**, in Gloversville, thus establishing the **Martin & Naylor** dry goods store.

John Martin was born in **Springfield, New Hampshire** on **August 29, 1847**, to **Reuben Martin** (1807 – 1851) and **Eliza A**. (nee **Langmaid**) **Martin** (Date of birth unknown – 1847).

John Martin's father passed away when John was less than four years old.

John was educated in the public schools of **Sutton, New Hampshire**, home of his grandfather, **Dr. William Martin**.

During the **American Civil War**, John was a member of **Co. E., Eight Regiment, Massachusetts Volunteer Militia**. John served from **July 14, 1864**, to **November 10, 1864**.

Following the War, Martin went west to **Kansas** where he engaged in farming and raising livestock.

Three years later, he headed back east to **Wakefield, Massachusetts**, where he went into the dry goods business with his brother, **William**. Later John bought out his brother's interest in the business and continued to operate it until **1879**.

That year, **1879**, he entered partnership with **H. H. Sturtevant** in **Zanesville, Ohio**. The business now went by the name of **Sturtevant & Martin**.

During this time, a young man by the name of **Edwin Charles Naylor** entered the employment of Sturtevant & Martin's firm.

On **November 8, 1881**, Mr. Martin married **Mary Wilder Adams** (1857 – 1910), a daughter of **Ezra Bartlett Adams** (1826 – 1914) and **Mary Lincoln** (nee **Wilder**) **Adams** (1826 – 1857).

John and **Mary Martin** would have two known children: **Grace Adams Martin** (1882 – 1959) and **Helen Wilder Martin** (1884 – Deceased).

In **1890**, John Martin left Zanesville, Ohio and headed to **Gloversville, NY**. Here he purchased the dry goods firm of **Dan Edwards & Son**. Next, Martin sent for Edwin C. Naylor and on **Sept. 15, 1890**, the mercantile firm of **Martin & Naylor** was formed.

In **1910**, John Martin's wife, **Mary** (age 52/53), died. She is buried at **Prospect Hill Cemetery**, Gloversville, NY.

John Martin (69) died on **January 17, 1917**, in **Lake Worth, Palm Beach, Florida**. He is buried at **Prospect Hill Cemetery**, Gloversville, NY.

With Martin's death, **Edwin C. Naylor** was elevated from **vice president** to **president** of the company, a position he held at the time of his death in **1950**.

Martin's son-in-law, **William Wemple Strong** (husband of Martin's daughter Helen Wilder), took over as the company's **vice president** of the firm. Strong had worked at the store for several years before the promotion. He held this position until he was killed during an ice storm in **1942**.

Upon her husband, William Wemple Strong's death, in **1942**, his widow **Helen Wilder** (nee **Martin**) **Strong** took over as the company's **vice president** and upon the death, in **1950**, of company president, **Edwin C. Naylor**, she became **president** of the firm with her son, **Wilder Strong**, becoming **vice president**.

Edwin Charles Naylor was born on **February 17, 1860**, in **Gettysburg, Darke County, Ohio** to **Charles Naylor** (1831 – 1901) and **Margaret B.** (nee **Harper**) **Naylor** (1832 – 1891).

Edwin attended public schools in Gettysburg until he was 15 years old, followed by advanced classes in a school at **Greenville, Darke County, Ohio**. Living at home, Edwin commuted back and forth to Greenville by a combination of freight and passenger train.

After a year at school in Greenville, Edwin entered the dry goods trade as an employee of the **Moore & Winner** dry goods store in **Greenville**. Here he was given free room and board plus $2 per week for his work.

After several years, he left the Moore & Winner concern, and became associated with the **Sturtevant & Martin** store in **Zanesville, Ohio**.

In **1890**, John Martin left Zanesville, Ohio and relocated to **Gloversville, NY,** where he purchased the dry goods firm of **Dan Edward & Son**. He then sent for **Edwin C. Naylor** and on

September 15, 1890, the firm of **Martin & Naylor** was formed.

Edwin was married to **Virginia S.** (nee **Lucas) Naylor** (1874 – 1962). The couple had no known children.

Edwin's wife, **Virginia**, was previously married to William B. Walker (1877 – 1908). They were married in **1903** and had **one** known son, **Arthur J. W. Naylor** (1904 – 1991).

At some point Arthur, keeping his last name Walker, also incorporated the last name Naylor, forming the name "**Arthur John Walker Naylor**."

Arthur would go on to marry **Marian Mabel Ferguson** (1909 – 1999), a daughter of **Dr. Joseph** and **Mable Azeida** (nee **McIndoe) Ferguson**. Arthur and Marian would have **one** known child: **Wendy Marian Walker Naylor Wood** (1944 – 2002).

Arthur W. Naylor, stepson of Edwin C. Naylor, joined the family business in **1929**, after graduating from the **School of Commerce** at **New York University**. He became **treasurer** of the firm in **1932** and purchased the business from **Mr. Helen Wilder Strong** in **June 1951**.

Edwin Charles Naylor died on **January 15, 1950** (89) at **Gloversville, NY**. He is buried at **Cromer Cemetery, Gettysburg, Darke Co., Ohio.**

Edwin's widow, **Virginia**, died on **December 11, 1962** (88) and is buried at **Ferndale Cemetery, Johnstown, Fulton Co., NY** beside her first husband, **William B. Walker.**

A portion of an article in **The Evening Telegram, Herkimer, NY, October 11,1961**, concerning **Genung's Inc.** buying the **H. G. Munger & Co**. and their store in **Herkimer**, reads, *Acquired Gloversville Store – In 1937, Munger's acquired Martin & Naylor department store in Gloversville, founded in 1890 and was one of the largest retail firms in northeastern New York. The Gloversville store was sold recently. Munger's also operated another store in Boonville, established in 1940. This store is now closed.*

In **October 1937**, when Munger's purchased **Martin & Naylor**, housed in the three-story **Getman Block** in Gloversville, the store continued to operate under the "**Martin & Naylor**" name.

Arthur John Walker Naylor (86) died on **July 24, 1991**. He is buried in **Ferndale Cemetery, Johnstown, Fulton Co., NY**. His widow, **Marian**, died on January 13, 1999 (89). She is also buried at Ferndale Cemetery.

According to Marian's obituary, she and her husband owned and operated the **Martin & Naylor Department Store**, Gloversville. Before her husband retired from the store, she opened **Wendy's Gift Shops** in **Mayfield** and **Ogunquit**. After she retired, she worked part-time for the **Hearthstone Town and Country** newspaper.

A headline in the **Leader-Herald** newspaper, **Gloversville, NY, Thursday, February 2, 1961**, read, *Parke Snow Chain from Massachusetts Buys Martin & Naylor Department Store.*

The article, in part, read, *Martin & Naylor Company, a Gloversville department store dating back to 1890, is under new management today. The store, operated since October of 1937, by H. G. Munger & Company, Inc., of Herkimer was sold yesterday to Parke Snow, Inc., a company which has been operating a chain of department stores, all in Massachusetts, since 1882, with its headquarters at Waltham, Mass.*

Charles A. Whipple, president and treasurer of Parke Snow announced today that Paul G. Miller, manager of the store under the Munger operation, will serve the new store as vice president and general manager. No personnel changes are contemplated. The store will take the name Parke Snow.

———————

In early **1940**, a third **Munger's store** emerged at **111 Main St.,** in **Boonville, NY.** This store would operate under the "**H. G. Munger & Co**." name.

The Boonville Herald newspaper, **January 25, 1940**, reported, *H. G. Munger & Co. To Open New Department Store in Boonville – Perry's Store to Close Doors After Many Years of Service* *"Perry's," a name which has been identified with the department store business in Boonville for nearly a half century, will continue as such no longer.*

Announcement was made Tuesday that Mrs. Lincoln Perry is retiring from business and that most desirable piece of property has been leased to H. G. Munger & Company of Herkimer. The transaction between the two firms was consummated on Monday.

Perry's Store will open its doors for the last time Saturday, Feb. 3, but beginning Friday, Jan. 24, and ending Saturday, Feb. 3, Perry's will conduct a storewide sale in order to close out completely their entire stock.

Executives of the Munger Company stated Tuesday that after extensive alterations to the Perry store, they will open there a branch of their Herkimer department store.

The Munger Company will open their new store in about six weeks with a complete line of women's and children's apparel and accessories, yard goods, domestics, linens, notions, men's furnishings, house furnishings and other small departments.

Perry's has been one of Boonville's finest stores since 1893. It was in that year that the late Lincoln Perry first opened a dry goods store in the Ready Block, Main Street, where the Palmore store is now located.

After a few years, Mr. Perry went into partnership with the late Harry Belknap. At the same time, they moved their store into the Herald Building where they conducted a successful business.

Mr. Belknap later sold out his interest in the firm and opened a grocery store where the Hess Pharmacy is now located.

Upon the death of Mr. Perry in 1917, his wife took over the business and has conducted the store to the present time.

The present store was built in 1912 on the site of the first Masonic Temple building and became a shopping center for a large area about Boonville.

Executives of Munger Company state that the Herkimer store has enjoyed considerable trade from Boonville and the north country area for many years, and they hope by establishing a branch here to better serve their customers and also make new friends in this section.

The Munger store celebrated its 70th anniversary last year by completely remodeling and modernizing its interior and is now one of the most modern, spacious and attractive stores in Central New York.

The store was founded by H. G. Munger in 1869 in a little one-room store in North Main Street, Herkimer, using only two clerks.

As the store grew, it changed its location, enlarged its space, opened new departments, until now it occupies three large floors of over 75,000 square feet of floor space, with more than 40 large departments and about 100 employees.

The late Henry G. Munger, founder of the store, was a farsighted and progressive merchant.

Starting his store at a period when most of women's apparel, laces, silks and many other items were brought to this country from abroad, he went to New York whenever large shipments were expected, bought shrewdly and sold wisely, building up a tremendous business.

After his death, the business was carried on for 10 years by his grandson, Henry M. Simmons, who died last year. Several members of the family are now interested in the Munger Company.

The store has always been famous for high quality, fair values and friendly service, and executives of the store state that the Boonville Munger store will be conducted on the same principles, and they expect to serve the people of the northern towns with the same success they have enjoyed in the Mohawk Valley.

The coming of the Munger Company to Boonville is like welcoming an old friend. Now that the vast resources of this fine organization are being brought to our doorstep, it is safe to say that they will be warmly received.

––––––––––––

According to **Boonville Town Historian**, **James S. Pitcher**, *On Thursday, April 14, 1940, an open house was held in the new Munger's Department Store with the first day of business occurring on Friday the 15th.*

The store, which was an extension of the highly successful Munger's Department Store in Herkimer offered its clients fine apparel for men, women and children, as well as household items ranging from China to floor coverings. At some point in time, the store became devoted exclusively to women's fashions and accessories. The store provided employment for many women in Boonville.

Continuing his history of the Boonville Munger's store, James writes in another document, In early 1940, the Perry Department Store building was leased to H. G. Munger, Inc., of Herkimer. Mrs. Doris Williams was the manager for several years, followed by George Kemp.

In the early 1950's, Mrs. Ann Higby was promoted from manager of the dress department to store manager.

The stately two-story store housed a large household department, dress department and millinery department on the second floor.

During the Christmas season, the second floor also displayed a large toy department.

The first floor had two very large plate glass windows, used for displays, also a jewelry department, lingerie department, notions, bedding, towels, etc.

Several local ladies were employed by Munger's including Dorothy Moonam, Ethel Stoffle, Ethel Elsaser, Florence Putney, Marjorie Phillips, Mary Daskewich, and Marie Jackson.

In 1955, Mungers joined in the Boonville Bicentennial celebration by having both windows elaborately decorated for the celebration. One window displayed a bridal party display, while the other depicted a bicentennial theme.

Munger's sponsored a contestant, Inez Higby, for the beauty pageant held during the bicentennial celebration. Inez Higby was crowned the Queen of the Bicentennial with Sandra Coahn and Shelly Kaiding as her attendants.

Munger's also sponsored a fashion show held at the Franjo Theater, in 1956, with Marie Jackson, Nancy Bartelotte, Jane Klosner, Joyce Presta and Inez Higby as models.

In 1960, the Munger's store was closed.

The **Utica Observer Dispatch**, Utica, NY, **February 24, 1960**, reported in part, ***Store Soon To Close – Boonville** – The local store of H. G. Munger & Co. is being closed, it was disclosed today. Leon Harris, general manager of Munger's, said today the store will be closed after a sale, now in progress, is completed. Harris added that the closing does not affect Munger's Herkimer store, the largest department store in that village. The Boonville department store has been operated by Munger's since 1940. The building which it occupies will be sold, Harris said.*

Following Munger's closing, several other stores, over the following years, occupied the building. The ones known are **Oliver's PFAFF Sewing Center & Kay Dee Co.**, **Western Auto**, and presently, since **1981**, **Capri Pizzeria**.

H. G. Munger & Co. 10/24/27
Buys Gloversville Store

H. G. Munger & Co. today announced acquisition of the well-known Martin & Naylor department store in Gloversville, founded in 1890 and one of the largest retail firms in northeastern New York.

Henry R. Jewett, president of Munger's, said the operation will be taken over Monday with closing of the purchase and continue under its present name as a wholly-owned subsidiary of the Munger company.

L. V. Harris, general manager of Munger's, said a close association has long existed between the two stores.

"When the founders were active," he said. "H. G. Munger and Edwin C. Naylor often met in New York on buying trips to discuss mutual problems. This neighborliness still continues."

Martin & Naylor, like Munger's, occupies three floors and a basement. It is identical in area to Munger's main store, built in 1918 after fire swept the business area here, with the same type of arcade entrance.

The Gloversville firm started when John Martin, a Zanesville, Ohio, merchant, purchased the D. M. Edwards store, and was soon joined on Sept. 15, 1890 by Naylor his former employe.

Naylor became president on Martin's death in 1917 and continued until he died in 1950 when Arthur Naylor, member of the firm since 1929 and treasurer since 1942 acquired sole ownership from Mrs. Helen Martin Strong, who had been associated with the store since 1942 when her husband, William Strong, was killed in an ice storm.

When Martin and Naylor was founded, it had 6,000 square feet of floor space, but the two partners and younger executives extended it to over 50,000. About 10 years ago, a $150,000 renovation project introduced new shopping conveniences and fixtures. The store serves an urban and rural population of 65,000.

The property, to be leased from the Getman Memorial Home, consists of the three-story building and a parking lot for about 35 vehicles in the rear. The store has approximately 70 employes.

Munger's, which recently enlarged its Herkimer store, also has operated another in Boonville since 1940. With 88 years in the department store field, Munger's are formulating plans for future growth of the Gloversville store, officials said.

PURCHASED BY LOCAL FIRM. The Martin & Naylor Department Store in Gloversville, founded in 1890, shown above, has been purchased by H. G. Munger & Co. of Herkimer. The new owners will take over operation Monday.

Name of Newspaper Not Listed
October 26, 1937
From the files of the Herkimer Co. Historical Society
Herkimer, Herkimer Co., NY
[Resized from Original]

CHAPTER FIFTEEN
H. G. MUNGER & CO. – THE WAR YEARS
[Munger's during World War II]

The **United States** entered **World War II** with the **December 7, 1941,** surprise attack on **Pearl Harbor** by the **Empire of Japan.**

On **December 8th**, the day after the Japanese attacked Peal Harbor, **President Franklin Roosevelt** delivered his "**Day of Infamy**" speech to the country. Following his speech, Congress declared war on Japan.

On **December 11, 1941**, Germany, being an ally of **Japan, declared war on the United States.** That same day, **America declared war on Germany.**

It wasn't long before food and other commodities were "**rationed**" to supply our troops with the needed **food, clothing** and **the other essentials** needed to fight a war.

The first item to be rationed was "**tires,**" beginning in **December 1941.**

Following that, the rationing of commodities was done in "**stages.**"

In May of **1942,** the rationing of **food** started with the rationing of **sugar.** Later, **coffee** was also on the list.

Government issued "**ration coupon books**" to the American public, which were needed to purchase certain "**rationed**" products in limited quantities.

By **November** of **1943,** the following items had been rationed: **typewriters, bicycles, shoes, rubber footwear, fuel oil and stoves.** Also, included on that list were the following: **Meat, lard, shortening and food oils, cheese, butter, margarine, processed foods, dried fruits, canned milk, firewood and coal, jams, jellies and fruit butter.**

As the **United States'** involvement in **World War II** pressed on in the **European** and **Pacific Theater,** back on the "**Home Front,**" **Munger's** continued as usual with a few notable exceptions: The most notable being that of the total elimination of all women's **silk** and **Nylon** stockings in **Munger's Lingerie Department.**

This lack of silk and Nylon stockings not only impacted Munger's, but also **all retailers** throughout the country.

At the time, **America's sole supplier of silk** was **Japan**. In **1941**, with America's **deteriorating** trade relations with Japan, **all shipments of silk were cut off to America**.

Nylon was invented in **1938** by the Dupont Co. as an **alternative** to silk. Although selling at the time for **$1.25** a pair (the same as silk), **Nylon** hosiery, unlike silk, was **shrink proof** and **moth resistant**, making them a hit among women everywhere.

On **February 11, 1942**, the **War Production Board** commandeered Dupont's stock of **Nylon.** From then on, Dupont's production of **Nylon** went solely to the "**War Effort**." During the War, Nylon went into the production of parachutes, among other wartime commodities.

The year **1944** was a notable year for **Munger's** Department Store. It was their **75th Anniversary** in business.

The store celebrated with **sales and promotions** during the entire month of **May**.

On **Monday, May 6, 1944**, **The Evening Telegram**, Herkimer, NY, ran the first of many   Munger's ads that month celebrating their **75th Anniversary** in business.

During this time, "**Munger's Fashion Report**" could be heard daily at **9:05 a.m**. over **WIBX** radio.

In **August** of **1945**, eight days after **Japan** surrendered, **Dupont** announced that it would **resume producing Nylon stockings** once again. Slowly, until **Dupont** returned to **full production**, **Nylons**, in **limited quantities**, returned to store shelves.

   It wouldn't be until **January** of **1946**, however, when Munger's **would start receiving** their shipments of **Nylons**.

   In the **fall of 1945**, **H. G. Munger & Co.** began construction of a **third-floor addition** to their **North Main St. Herkimer, NY** building. At the time, the Munger's building consisted of a **basement** (lower level) and **two upper floors**.

   The Evening Telegram, Herkimer NY, **September 12, 1945**, read in part, *Munger's Store Planning Addition of Third Story* – *Post-war expansion plans, which will include the construction of a third story in the main building, are already underway at the H. G. Munger & Co. department store, according to a statement made today by Leon V. Harris, manager.*

According to the program laid out for the enlargement of the store, of which work will be started in the near future, the new floor will house various enlarged home furnishing departments, including a large floor Covering Department and an expanded Curtain and Drapery Department.

These departments, Harris said, will be moved from the present second floor. The business office, including credit, control, advertising and the manager's office will also be transferred to the third floor.

"Fashion Floor" Planned – In reality, the additional floor will give the Munger company four stories in which to do business. This included the basement.

The second floor, after the addition has been completed, will then be made into a "fashion floor" in which will be located an enlarged Women's and Misses' Apparel Shop, Girls' Shop, Teen-age Shop, Boys' Shop, California Shop, Corsets, Shoes and Millinery.

Harris also said that plans are being made to open a Beauty Salon, Photograph Studio and an Optical Department.

The basement space will also be enlarged by relocation of lockers and stock rooms, to give space to a new "Electric City." The store will open a department of General Electric appliances which will include a model electric kitchen and laundry and will feature all the new electric devices which have been designed to make homes more comfortable and to shorten hours of labor.

The Evening Telegram, Herkimer, NY, October 26, 1945, reported in part, **Munger Employees Set For V-Bond Campaign** – Munger store employees have volunteered their services to help put over the Victory War Loan campaign, which opens Monday, according to plans announced here today by Leon V. Harris, store manager.

The employees have been again divided into six teams, each headed by a captain, Harris said. All members of the team selling the greatest amount in War Bonds during the campaign will be rewarded with two days' vacation with pay, sometime between Jan. 1st and Feb. 15th.

In addition, an employee on each of the other teams who sells the greatest amount of bonds will also receive two days' vacation with pay. To qualify for a vacation award, a team member must sell at least $500 in bonds.

In a bulletin to employees, Harris pointed out that the Victory Loan was important, first to hospitalize the wounded of World War II, to feed and clothe the men still overseas and furnish transportation to return them home; and second, to satisfy our obligations as a nation, to pay the costs of war and veteran assistance which by June 30th will have reached $335,000,000,000.

A **Munger's New Year's Eve** advertisement, appearing in **The Evening Telegram,** Herkimer, NY, **December 31, 1945,** read in part, ***Munger's 1946 Plans***: A New Fourth Floor! A New Fashion Floor! Remodeled Basement! A big "Electric City!" The addition of an Optical Shop, Beauty Salon and Photograph Studio!

A Munger's ad in **The Evening Telegram, Herkimer, NY, January 25, 1946**, read in part, ***We'll have them! But so far, shipments of Nylons have been small and totally inadequate to supply the demand – so…. Until Further Notice, Munger's Is Adopting the Following Plan of Distributing NYLON STOCKINGS – For These Practical Reasons***: *1 We want to be as fair as is humanly possible to all of our customers. 2. We want local customers and out-of-town customers to be treated alike. 3. We want both charge customers and cash customers to be treated alike.*

So, Until Further Notice, This Is the Munger Plan for Selling NYLONS. Below you will find a coupon. Fill it out completely, including your size (very important) and mail it to us at once. All coupons will be filed and filled in order of their receipt. As soon as a quantity of Nylons is available, postcards will be mailed in the order received to all the customers for whom we have stockings available, telling them when to present the card at our hosiery department in order to purchase one pair of Nylons.

Don't ask for stockings by mail. Don't phone. Don't send us any money. Don't ask for Nylons – none will be sold over the counter. Coupons accepted by mail only.

The Evening Telegram, Herkimer, NY, **April 2, 1946**, read in part, ***Local Construction Unhit by Material Restrictions*** *– Four projects, estimated to cost more than $100,000 and designed to improve Herkimer as a trading and recreation center, coupled with industrial expansion plans of several local firms, today established one of the biggest building booms in the village's history.*

The Munger store project is well underway and will not be hit by restrictions on materials. The work started last fall. The third-floor addition already presents an idea of how the building will look when the work has been completed.

Stairwells, Shaft Ready *– The face or Main St. wall has been erected and the open window frames await plate glass. Workmen are now placing the roof over the steel framework. The side and rear walls are 75 per cent up.*

Stairwells are in and the elevator shaft extension is also complete. Leon V. Harris, store manager, said he expects the entire project, including a complete renovation of the second floor, to be finished by midsummer.

The new floor, he said, will provide 14,000 square feet of space, thus making Munger's the largest department store in the Mohawk Valley. The main offices will be moved from the second floor to the top floor and an optical shop and beauty salon will be established on the second floor.

On **May 7, 1945**, the "unconditional surrender" of **Germany** was signed.

An article in **The Evening Telegram,** Herkimer NY, **June 1, 1946**, read in part, ***Renovating Plans Here Await Building Materials*** *– Herkimer merchants today indicated they eagerly await materials needed for putting into action plans for renovating their establishments.*

The completion of a third floor on Munger's Department Store was held up by the winter weather, Leon Harris, manager, declared. "But it's coming along nicely now," Harris said, "and when it's finished, it will add 13,500 square feet to our store. I guess it should be ready by September. Our other two floors are being completely revamped.

Munger's **unceremoniously** opened their new **third floor** in time for **Thanksgiving** and the start of the **Christmas season** that year, **1946**. An ad in **The Evening Telegram, Herkimer, NY, November 21, 1946**, headlined ***Christmas Gift Shops Open on Four Floors!***

On **September 2, 1945**, the **Empire of Japan** "unconditionally" surrendered to the **United States,** ending **World War II**.

"We're with you, Uncle Sam!"

Munger's Complies with Government Regulations to Help Win the War!

- **We've Posted Cost-of-Living Commodities**
  According to government instructions we posted a list of cost of living commodities in every department as early as May 1st!

- **We've Listed March Ceiling Prices**
  At the request of OPA—we have ready for your inspection, March ceiling prices on every item in stock!

- **We're Conserving Tires and Gasoline —**
  At government request, we've reduced deliveries to conserve tires and gasoline—but arranged schedules to give you good service just the same!

- **We've Eliminated Special Deliveries**
  We've eliminated pick-ups of return merchandise and special deliveries, except in case of emergency.

- **We're Conserving Paper, Twine, etc.**
  We're thriftily saving paper, twine, paper clips, rubber bands—doing our share for victory!

- **We're Following Government Credit Regulations**
  But you may still use your regular charge account and we still maintain for your convenience, our Budget Plan and Lay Away Plan—ask about them

- **We're Promoting Sale of War Bonds and Stamps**
  Munger's has been designated as an issuing agent of U. S. War Bonds—buy them at our Main Office—Second Floor—help send tanks, planes, ships.

- **We've Given Windows to Patriotic Displays**
  Our window of "Heroes All" (photographs of Herkimer County men in service), drew crowds of interested people for four days in a row!

- **We're Constantly Urging People to Save!**
  Save what you have—Munger's will repair, reupholster, refinish your furniture, mend your rugs, lay linoleum for long wear, make slip covers, draperies, spreads to make your home cheerful during these trying days!

"Buy Only What You Need
Save on What You Buy"—at

MUNGER'S
HERKIMER

MUNGER'S
HERKIMER

We'll have them! But so far, shipments of Nylons have been small and totally inadequate to supply the demand—so . . .

Until Further Notice
Munger's Is Adopting the
Following Plan of Distributing

NYLON
STOCKINGS

For These Practical Reasons

1—We want to be as fair as is humanly possible to *all* our customers.

2—We want local customers and out-of-town customers to be treated alike.

3—We want charge customers and cash customers to be treated alike.

So, Until Further Notice,
This Is the Munger Plan for
Selling NYLONS

Below you will find a coupon. Fill it out completely including your size (very important) and mail to us at once. All coupons will be filed and filled in order of their receipt. As soon as a quantity of Nylons is available, postcards will be mailed in the order received to all of the customers for whom we have stockings available, telling them when to present the card at our hosiery department in order to purchase one pair of Nylons.

- Don't ask for stockings by mail.
- Don't phone.
- Don't send us any money.
- Don't ask for Nylons—none will be sold over the counter.

H. G. MUNGER and CO.—Herkimer, N. Y.
Please notify me when I may come to purchase one pair of NYLON Stockings.

NAME ....
ADDRESS ....
TOWN or CITY ....
I Wear Size ....2nd Choice ....
(Please Print)

Coupons Accepted by Mail Only!

Evening Telegram
Herkimer, NY
January 25, 1946
[Resized from Original]

The Evening Telegram, Herkimer, NY
Monday, May 8, 1944
[Resized from Original]

Munger's

of HERKIMER
and BOONVILLE

A Store of Today and Tomorrow...
....with 75 Years of Yesterdays

The prestige and confidence which MUNGER'S possesses are valuable assets built by three quarters of a century of service to discriminating shoppers of the Mohawk Valley.

MUNGER'S, which is independently owned and operated by alert management, is a store of today and tomorrow because during its long years of establishment, it has kept pace with progress...

> —*by providing fashion-right quality apparel and accessories for women, misses and children.*

> —*by being first in promoting new ideas in home furnishing—to make living easier and happier.*

> —*by modern methods of store operation*

> —*and by working co-operatively with leading manufacturers and wholesalers.*

MUNGER'S sponsored merchandise has the prestige which goes with the store name and the acceptance that the store's endorsement creates.

MUNGER'S has a reputation for quality and dependability—MUNGER'S has a name famous for fashion leadership since 1869.

THE ORIGINAL MUNGER STORE was established in Herkimer in 1869—four years after the close of the Civil War—in the days of the hoopskirts and shawls. The first store contained only two rooms —but to this store the founder brought the finest merchandise imported to America from across the seas!

THE PRESENT STORE in North Main Street, Herkimer, contains over two acres of floor space in its three floors. A list of patrons over the span of years since 1869 includes families which have contributed much to the glorious history of the Mohawk Valley.

MUNGER'S STORE at BOONVILLE is now only four years old—but growing fast!

MUNGER'S---HAS FASHION PRESTIGE---IN THE MOHAWK VALLEY

Addition to H. G. Munger Store Herkimer, N.Y. Rogers & Butler Architects
[Architectural concept painting of Munger's facade after 3rd floor is added]
3rd floor (top) finished and opened to the public in 1946.
[Resized from original.]

...And She Told Me to Get It at MUNGERS!

Santa can keep a secret—a nod and a wink is absolutely as far as he will go! So we don't know what the lady wanted—we only know she was emphatic in specifying MUNGER'S as the place to choose her Christmas gift. Of course, it's no secret at all that the nicest gifts, the gifts that reflect real discrimination come from this great store—bigger and busier than ever, now with Christmas gift shops on FOUR FLOORS!

Free Parking in Rear of Store

MUNGER'S---Herkimer

Famous for Gifts Since 1869!

CHAPTER SIXTEEN
H. G. MUNGER & CO. – THE NINETEEN FIFTIES

In **June** of **1950**, the United States was no **longer** at war. That year Munger's observed their **81st Anniversary** in business. An article in the **Evening Telegram**, **May 29, 1950,** read in part, ***Munger's Store to Mark 81st Anniversary June*** – *Munger's Department Store, widely known Herkimer landmark since shortly after the Civil War, will observe its 81st anniversary June 1st with a sale lasting to June 10th.*

The **Utica Daily Press, March 6, 1953**, reported, ***MUNGER's "WOMEN'S DAY"*** – *Women of the H. G. Munger & Co. store, Herkimer, assumed active management of the store yesterday during the annual "Women's Day." Male employees dressed as women were around the store.*

The **Evening Telegram, Herkimer, NY, January 3, 1956**, reported, ***Munger Story on Times Square Sign*** – *On Jan. 5th, from dusk to 1 a.m., Herkimer will take over Times Square in New York City. At that time, the giant spectacular at 42nd St. and 7th Ave. will flash the Munger Story.*

The sign is the biggest in Times Square. It is 237 feet long, nearly as long as a football field, 20 feet high and has a tower that soars an additional 58 feet into the sky. In the center of the sign, a huge motor-graph, consisting of a bank of electric bulbs 60 feet long and five feet high, carries a 100-word moving message in lights, like the one on the Times Square building, directly across the street.

The story of Munger's as Central New York's trading center, located in Herkimer, gateway to the north country, will be flashed throughout the night and until 1 a.m. Arrangements for the spectacular showing in the Great White Way has been made through the Milium Corporation which has singled out H. G. Munger & Co. as one of the outstanding stores in America and one that has been closely allied with the promotion of Millum "warmth without weight" Linings in women's apparel and by the yard.

Blowups of the sensational sign will appear in Munger's windows within a few days, L. V. Harris, manager of Munger's announced. This is a novel venture in publicity for Munger's. "The appearance of Munger's name on Times Square's largest sign will cause a definitely favorable reaction in the market, and with the manufacturers with whom Munger's deals with," he said. "It will tend to give added stature to a small-town store and enable it to stand shoulder to shoulder with the giants of the country. Fine manufacturers are constantly on the alert for fine stores to promote their merchandise and through the wide publicity that will attend this sign, more doors of trade will be opened wider."

Munger's is perhaps the first small-town store in the country to take over the very heart of the Gay White Way, and the countless thousands that will view the sign will come to know something of the attractions of Herkimer, NY.

The **Utica Observer Dispatch**, Utica, NY, ran a Munger's ad on **February 13, 1957**, which stated, *"In* keeping with the changing times, ***Munger's Will Close All Day Mondays beginning Feb. 18th.***

For 87 years, H. G. Munger & Co. has grown and progressed by keeping abreast of the times.

Today, men and women in industry, offices, banks and professions enjoy the benefits of a 5-day week. Department stores, too, have been closing on Mondays in such cities as Providence, Hartford, Schenectady and many others.

In adopting the 5-day work week at Munger's, we break with tradition to keep in step with the growing trend and the "American Way."

It goes without saying that the people who serve you here at Munger's will be happier about a 5-day week with no loss in pay. They will find in this an urge to serve you even better during the five days we'll be open.

Open: *Tuesdays, Wednesdays & Thursdays 10 to 5:30. Fridays, 10 to 9:00 and on Saturdays, 10 to 5:30.*

In making this decision, Munger's again demonstrates the kind of leadership that has come down to us from the store's founder, H. G. Munger…the leadership that constitutes a beam of light to keep us on our course as we chart the future.

 In **1957**, Munger's, who at the time was operating their **furniture department** from the second floor of the **Grogan Building**, located directly to the right of their store, by means of an archway between the two buildings, expanded their furniture department into the first floor by means of a second entrance, between the two buildings at street level.

Before this, the **W. T. Grant** store for years had leased this space from Munger's who had purchased the building back in late **1922**. The **Grand Opera House** once operated on the building's third (top) floor.

The **Evening Telegram, June 18, 1957**, Herkimer, NY, reported in part, ***Munger's Expands Store to Adjacent Building** – H. G. Munger & Co. will expand its present store to take over the entire three-story building to the south and add 7, 700 square feet to its present street floor space, L. V. Harris, manager, announced today.*

Signifying faith in Herkimer as a business center and the future of the central Mohawk Valley, the announcement said the expansion will add 64% to Munger's present North Main St. frontage.

Work has already begun on extensive alterations to join the main floors of the two stores into one great shopping center, the manager said.

Entrances from one building to the other will be provided by breaking through the wall.

An entire new front, matching the black Carrara glass of the present store, will be installed on the street floor of the building occupied by W. T. Grant Co. for 23 years, Harris said.

This will include a massive display window with recessed entrance to the store through glass doors, he added.

Installation of an elevator in the rear of the building, a sprinkler system, modern lighting and a carpeted floor are other details of the plan.

The newly added floor space will also connect with Munger's second floor, where its furniture department and model rooms are now located. The work is under the direction of G. Willard Blauvelt, Herkimer contractor.

Harris said the expansion program marked the ninth time H. G. Munger & Co. has required additional space since its founding in 1869.

Plans for opening of the new building, acquired by Munger's in 1922, from the late Thomas Grogan, former mayor, called for completion of the work by early fall, Harris said.

Munger's Store Begins 81st Year in Herkimer

Herkimer — When the H. G. Munger Store opened its doors this morning it began it's 81st year as one of Herkimer County's leading department stores.

Marking the observance will be an anniversary sale, announces Leon V. Harris, starting Thursday morning.

It was just 81 years ago that Henry G. Munger opened a little one-room dry goods store in Main St., here.

From that small beginning has grown the present four-floor modern department store.

The first store had only two clerks but it drew trade so rapidly that Munger was soon forced to seek larger quarters.

At six different times he moved his store as growth and expansion demanded it. In 1917 a disastrous fire which destroyed the heart of Herkimer's business section, also leveled the store.

Although then 70 years old, Munger began to plan for a new and larger store. The present building was the result.

In 1933, at Munger's death, management of the business passed to his grandson, Henry M. Simmons, who began a modernization program.

His untimely death in an auto accident in 1938 delayed the work. But in 1939, under the direction of the present manager, Leon V. Harris, the plans were carried out.

The store is believed to be one of the few establishments in Central New York which has remained through the years under family ownership.

President of the company is Guernsey R. Jewett, White Plains, son-in-law of the founder, and vicepresident is Charles Belmer, husband of Munger's granddaughter. Bruce Steele of Burlington, Vt., a grandson, is also a vicepresident.

The public service policy set by the founder has been carried down the years, Harris emphasizes.

May 28, 1950

No Source Given

[Resized from Original]

Munger's Building North Main St. Herkimer, NY Circ. 1950's/'60's
[Resized from original.]

an announcement

☞ in keeping with the changing times

MUNGER'S
will close
all day
MONDAYS

beginning **MON. Feb. 18th**

open

Tuesdays	Wednesdays	Thursdays	Fridays	Saturdays
10 to 5:30	10 to 5:30	10 to 5:30	10 to 9:00	10 to 5:30

For 87 years, H. G. Munger & Co. has grown and progressed by keeping abreast of the times.

Today, men and women in industry, offices, banks and professions enjoy the benefits of a 5-day week. Department stores, too, have been closing on Mondays in such cities as Providence, Hartford, Schenectady and many others.

In adopting the 5-day work week at Munger's we break with tradition to keep in step with the growing trend and the "American way."

It goes without saying that the people who serve you here at Munger's will be happier about a 5-day week with no loss in pay. They will find in this an urge to serve you even better during the five days we'll be open.

In making this decision, Munger's again demonstrates the kind of leadership that has come down to us from the store's founder, H. G. Munger . . . the leadership that constitutes a beam of light to keep us on our course as we chart the fu...

H. G. MUNGER & CO., Herkimer and Boonville

Utica Observer – Dispatch
Utica, NY
February 13, 1957
[Resized from Original]

CHAPTER SEVENTEEN
ELEVATOR GOING UP
[Finding Your Way Through the H. G. Munger & Co. Store]

Way back when, spending the day shopping at a department store was considered an exciting event to look forward to: An experience if you will.

This was a time when many people from outlying rural areas made it into town only two or three times a year, if that, to stock up on supplies or provisions.

These rural folks would make a day of shopping, buying in large quantities to last through the long periods between trips.

And, of course, the city folks also delighted in spending time in the store looking over the latest in fashions and dry goods.

The **H. G. Munger & Co**. store originally consisted of a **lower level** (basement) and **two upper** floors. A **third floor** was added in **1946**. For customers trying to get from one floor to the next, with an armful of packages, was a chore.

With the building of their new store, in **1918**, a passenger elevator was installed, to alleviate the above problem.

According to the internet blog "**Throughout History – A Blog about Antiques and History,**" *early elevators were manually operated. Gates to the elevator car and the shaft were opened and closed by hand. And the elevator cars themselves were manually operated. A lever and switch were pulled to send the car up or down, and at varying speeds.*

The first elevators were controlled by one of the passengers. It was up to them to park at the elevator level with the opening in the shaft.

As this was not a skill everyone had, buildings with elevators soon employed elevator operators to guide elevators and their passengers, up and down in safety.

In department stores with elevators, elevator operators often acted as guides, explaining what products could be found on each floor, which shopping departments could be found where, and what special offers or sales were going on in any given department(s).

The early elevators lacked dials to tell the customers or operator what floor they were on. Thus, the operator (having memorized the floors and what was on them) would call out the direction of travel as well, as a courtesy to passengers.

"Ground floor! Lobby, restaurant, hairdressers, barbers and bookshop! Going up! First Floor! Men's suits, hats, shirts, socks, ties and accessories! Going up! Second Floor! Ladies' wear, handbags, shoes, hats, gloves, scarves, make-up and perfume!"

Store Directories were also prominently placed throughout the store telling customers what floor a certain category of merchandise was located on.

Back in the early days, a seat was provided, in the elevator, for the conductor who operated the lift. This eliminated the need for the conductor to be on their feet for long periods at a time.

Although not currently in working condition, the old Munger's passenger elevator, with its glass fronts encased in an ornate wooden façade, still exists, waiting to be repaired and placed back in service.

Today it may seem inconceivable to think that customers once relied on the assistance of an "**elevator operator**" to take them from one floor to another in the store. Back then, however, it was commonplace.

Those days, unfortunately, are **sadly lost** when it comes to the modern-day department store.

Former employee **Tim Adam** was one of the last to hold the job description of a "**passenger elevator operator**" in the old Munger's building.

As Tim would probably tell you, "**The job had its ups and downs**."

STORE DIRECTORY

	FLOOR			FLOOR
A			**J**	
Aprons	1	Jewelry	1
Art Needlework	1	Junior Shop	1
B			**L**	
Beauty Salon	2	Lamps	Down & 3
Beds	3	Leather Goods	1
Blankets	1	Linens	1
Blouses	1	Lingerie	2
Books	1	Luggage	1
Boy Scouts	2		
Boys' Shop	2	**M**	
		Men's Clothing	1
C			Men's Furnishings	1
Candy	1	Men's Gifts	1
Carpets	3	Millinery	2
Candle Shop	Down	Mirrors	Down & 3
China	Down		
Closet Shop	1	**N**	
Coats	2	Neckwear	1
Cosmetics	1	Notions	1
Curtains	1		
		O	
D			Offices	3
Draperies	1		
Dresses – Better	2	**P**	
Dresses – Budget	2	Patterns	1
Dresses – Pin Money	1	Pictures	1 & 3
Dress Goods	1	Piece Goods	1
		Pin Money Dresses	1
E			
Electrical Appliances	Down	**R**	
Embroidery Goods	1	Radios	3
		Raincoats	2
F			Records	1
Fabrics	1	Ribbons	1
Furniture	3		
Furs	2	**S**	
Fur Storage	2	Service Desk	1
Foundations	1 & 2	Shoes	1
		Silverware	Down
G			Slipcovers	1
Gift Shop	Down	Sportswear	1
Girl Scouts	2	Sporting Goods	1
Girls' Shop	2	Stationery	1
Glassware	Down	Suits	2
Gloves	1		
Greeting Cards	1	**T**	
		Toys	2
H			Television	3
Handbags	1		
Handkerchiefs	1	**U**	
Housecoats – Robes	2	Umbrellas	1
Housewares	Down		
Hosiery	1	**V**	
		Vacuum Cleaners	Down
I			
Infants	2	**W**	
Infants' Furniture	2	Watch & Jewelry Repair	1
		Window Shades	1

Photocopy of an original Munger's Directory
Circa. 1950's/'60's
[Resized from Original]

*The term "DOWN" under the heading "FLOOR" refers to the "Lower Level" or "Basement." The term "Pin Money" refers to a "small amount of money."

Original
Munger's Passenger Elevator
Lower/Basement Level
Installed during 1917/'18 construction

CHAPTER EIGHTEEN
H. G. MUNGER & COMPANY SOLD

[The H. G. Munger & Co. Sold to Genung's Inc. – The Store Will Retain "Munger" Name]

For over **ninety-two years**, starting in **May** of **1869**, the Munger's family had been involved in the ownership of "**H. G. Munger & Co.**" and of its department store in downtown **Herkimer, NY**.

That all changed in **October** of **1961**, when **Genung's Inc.**, operating a chain of department stores in **New York** and **Connecticut**, under the "Genung" name, purchased "**H. G. Munger & Co.**"

An article in the **October 11, 1961, The Evening Telegram, Herkimer, NY** read in part, *Genung's Inc. Buys H. G. Munger & Co. – Acquistion of the H. G. Munger & Co., Herkimer's widely known 92-year-old department store, by Genung's Incorporated, a New York & Connecticut chain, was announced today.*

Leon V. Harris, manager of Munger's since 1938, advised the store's department buyers late yesterday after the sale had been completed in New York by the heads of the two firms.

The joint announcement by Henry Jewett, president of Munger's and Herbert N. Miles, president of Genung's, bring to fourteen the number of stores in Genung's expanding chain.

The amount involved in the transfer was not disclosed. Reports of the impending acquisition have been current for two weeks.

Genung's started in 1897 in Mt. Vernon, NY. Now they also have stores in White Plains, Yonkers, Tarrytown, Peekskill, Danbury, Norwalk, Meriden, Ridgefield and New London.

In addition, the firm owns southern Connecticut's largest department store, Howland's in Bridgeport and the Globe in Suffern and Stern's, Middletown.

*Genung's plans to **continue the H. G. Munger & Co**. name and will acquire the entire operation except the furniture department, which occupies three floors of adjoining, former Grogan Block, owned by the Munger's Holding Co., which expects to lease the building.*

The announcement said Genung's will offer merchandise in the popular to better price lines and feature brand names.

Robert Caskey, of Genung's management staff, will be the new store manager, succeeding Harris who said he will retire Nov. 1st after 56 years with Munger's. No other changes in operation or personnel are contemplated after the new owners take over on the same date, the announcement said.

Genung's president added that Munger's reputation for reliability and friendly customer service, developed by the store's founder and his successors were valuable assets which Genung's would strive in every way to preserve.

"We are looking forward," Millea said, "to a long, pleasant association with the people of the Herkimer area."

Genung's sales volume reportedly is in excess of $16,000,000. Munger's approximates $1,000,000 annually.

In the column to the right of the Genung" article is featured an article on **Leon V. Harris**, the retiring manager of "**H. G. Munger & Co.**" department store in Herkimer.

The article read, **L. V. Harris to Retire as Store Manager** – *Leon V. Harris, 325 Margaret St., manager of the H. G. Munger & Co. since 1938 and an employe of the store for 56 years, is retiring Nov. 1st, he said today.*

The announcement coincided with the acquisition of the store by Genung's Incorporated, New York and Connecticut chain, from the Munger family.

Mr. and Mrs. Harris have sold their home and are moving to Ilion, where they have purchased a residence at 9 Sunset Ave.

Before becoming manager in 1938, Harris filled almost every position in the store since 1905, when as a 15-year-old lad from the Newport farm area, he came to Herkimer by train and was engaged by Mr. Munger as an errand boy.

Within a week he was promoted to the service department, later took correspondence courses in window trimming and advertising to qualify for this combined post, and subsequently became buyer for the draperies, furniture and other departments.

After fire destroyed the store in 1917, he helped lay plans for the present building. The architects combined his ideas for the location of various departments. His tube system for sales slips to the cashier, still unchanged, was adopted intact.

He personally supervised and planned all later alterations in the store's expansion. The latest addition of a third floor, on the main building, was accomplished economically by direct purchase of all building materials.

During his long service, he was closely identified with the development and growth of the 92 year old enterprise, which now occupied nearly two acres of space in three buildings and employs nearly 100.

He became store manager on the death of Henry M. Simmons, grandson of the founder.

Harris is a past master of Herkimer Masonic Lodge, past president of the Herkimer Service Club, and a former director of the National Retail Dry Goods Assn., smaller stores division.

He was the guest of honor at a testimonial dinner given by company officials at the Mohawk Valley Country Club in 1956 to mark over half a century of service.

Mrs. Harris, the former Iva Bowen, is a member of Myrtie OES Chapter and both are members of the First Methodist Church. They were married Sept. 23, 1908, at the home of the bride in Herkimer. They have a daughter, Mrs. William Bleau, Mohawk, and two grandchildren.

Leon V. Harris, 88, died on **October 16, 1978**, in **Mohawk General Hospital**. His wife, Iva, had preceded him in death on **October 7, 1973**. They are both buried at **Oak Hill Cemetery**, Herkimer, NY.

Leon's obituary, which appeared in **The Evening Times, Herkimer, NY, October 16, 1978**, states that *Mr. Harris was first employed by the former Munger's store in 1905. In 1929, he became assistant manager, and in 1939 was appointed manager and treasurer, retiring in 1961.*

For all intent and purposes, the original **H. G. Munger & Co.** department store, in downtown Herkimer, NY, **ceased to exist** following the October 1961 purchase by Genung's Inc. No longer in the hands of the Munger family, the store was now "**Munger's**" in name only.

On **July 7, 1964**, Genung Inc. broke ground in the **New Hartford Shopping Center**, New Harford, NY (outside of Utica, NY) for the construction of a **50,000 square foot** Munger's Department Store. The new store was to employ **125 people** and was expected to be ready to open by the **spring** of **1965.**

On **Thursday, April 22ⁿᵈ, 1965**, Munger's opened their store in the **New Hartford Shopping Center**, in North Utica, NY. Today **JOANN Fabric and Crafts** and **Ollies** discount store occupy the space.

During this time, **spring 1965**, several Munger newspaper advertisements incorrectly listed Munger's as located in **Herkimer, Utica** and **Little Falls, NY**. While it is correct that Munger's operated a store in **Herkimer**, the "**Utica**" location should have read "**New Hartford**" and as for a Munger's in "**Little Falls**," according to **Mary Ann Terzi**, of the **Little Falls Historical Society**, Little Falls, NY, there is **no listing** in any of the **Little Falls Business Directories**, during this period, to substantiate the claim.

Author's Notes:

   No one who I have talked with or interviewed for this book **can remember** that there was ever a "**Munger's**" in **Little Falls.**

   In **1968**, Genung's Inc. was purchased by **Supermarket General**, a holding company (later becoming **Pathmark**). The new owners continued to allow the "**Munger's**" name to appear on the building above its entrance.

   By the end of the decade of the '60's, **1969** to be exact, what should have been a shining moment in the history of H. G. Munger's Department Store, with the celebration of their **100**th **Anniversary** in business, **went totally unnoticed** by the local newspaper and the store itself.

Munger's

NOW WE ARE TWO

Munger's, Herkimer and

.....THE NEW MUNGER'S, NEW HARTFORD

Opens Thursday April 22nd, at 10 A.M.

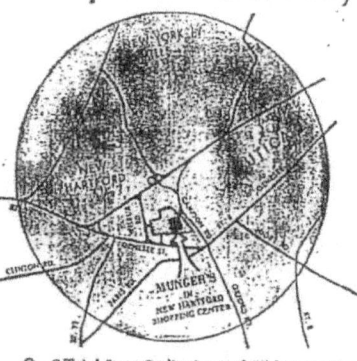

This is Munger's, New Hartford . . . a completely new and beautiful store dedicated to you, our discriminating customers. Munger's has always meant service, friendliness, experience, quality and respected brand names. These vital concepts will continue as part of the policies at Munger's, New Hartford. You will enjoy shopping at the new Munger's — designed with "you" in mind. You will find the newest, the most fashionable and unique merchandise for yourself, your family and your home, from the four corners of the world. It's an auspicious occasion, this new era of shopping convenience at Munger's, New Hartford . . . and we cordially invite you to be our honored guests!

- Official Store Dedication and Ribbon Cutting Ceremony at 10 A.M.
- Informal Fashion Showing
- Music by the Starlight Trio
- Special Broadcast over WIBX
- And More !

You'll find we're very easy to get to and our good neighbors in the New Hartford Shopping Center are a variety of stores so you can shop easily for all your needs at one time.

ENJOY SHOPPING AT MUNGER'S IN THE NEW HARTFORD SHOPPING CENTER
OPEN MONDAY, THURSDAY AND FRIDAY NIGHTS TIL 9 P.M.

The Clinton Courier
Clinton, NY
1965
[Resized from Original]

View of Women's Department of Munger's New Hartford Store

Munger's Manager Caskey and Assistant Manager Newman

Munger's Newest Store Opens Thursday

By BARBARA JONES

Herkimer's oldest and largest department store will be represented in Oneida County beginning Thursday when the Munger-Genung Co. opens its newest branch in the New Hartford shopping center.

Munger's New Hartford, will be the 25th department store in a group that maintains outlets in New York State, Connecticut and New Jersey.

A dedication beginning at 10 a. m. will signal the opening Thursday.

Fashion - conscious customers will be greeted by a majestic world of the latest merchandise artistically and conveniently displayed in the one-floor store.

* * *

ROBERT D. CASKEY, newly appointed general manager, said the store "introduces a new era of shopping convenience."

"Promoting fashion is our main concern."

said Caskey during a preview tour of the store. He said a two-year study of marketing and buying habits of local consumers revealed a need for a quality family apparel store.

"We found the area had a surplus of discount department stores but nothing for the discriminating customer in the middle and upper income brackets. The discount houses promote price . . . our policy is to promote high fashion," said Caskey.

The 50,000-square-foot building is divided into eight major departments: women's dresses, accessories (cosmetics, millinery, hosiery, handbags, jewelry and gloves), sportswear, intimate fashions and lingerie, children's clothes for infants to teens, men's fashions, shoes for the family and household furnishings.

* * *

ACCENT has been placed on the informal Mohawk Valley living. Utilizing this concept of informality, the store features two sportswear departments, one for misses and the other for the junior figure. Each department carries a complete line of coordinated separates, swimwear and beach accessories.

The female shopper can purchase a "pin money dress" (a Munger's creation for patio and grocery shopping) or a formal gown in the women's apparel section. There are 52 fitting rooms in the store. Inventory is valued at $1.5 million.

Located near the entrance is the men's

department. Suits, coats, sportswear and jewelry—are available for junior boys, preps and men.

One of the most popular departments probably will be the household section. Collections of china, glassware and small electrical appliances make a galaxy of wedding and bridal shower gifts.

A bridal registry will record brides-to-be preferences in china, silverware, linens and glassware. On opening day, two representatives of Bride's Magazine, Miss Tina Schafer and Miss Jean Luban, will begin the registry service.

The decor and interior decorations are neat, neat and in good taste. Utica architect Frank Delle Cese designed the $300,000 building. New York City firm of Copeland-Novak-Israel did the interior decorating, estimated at $750,000.

* * *

INDIRECT LIGHTING complements the predominantly blue, green and gold colors. Attractive hand-painted murals of carnations, butterflies and flowers abound in the children's department. Abstract hexagon patterns brighten the display walls. The art work was done by William Hankinson.

Caskey said the faces of the mannequins are likenesses of real models. He pointed out one figure with Sophia Loren's face.

The Munger's store chain began in a one-room dry goods store in Main Street, Herkimer, in 1870. In 1961, it was sold to Genung's of White Plains.

CHAPTER NINETEEN
CLOSING TIME – THE END OF AN ERA
[The Munger's Name Comes Down – September 1970]

It was once said that the proudest moment for any business, of years gone by, was when the freshly painted sign, bearing the name of the new establishment, was hung over the entrance. The saddest was when, years later, that same sign came down.

That sad day came in **September 1970**, for the old building which had proudly displayed the name "**Munger's**" over its entrance since **1918** (along with its other previous locations along the way).

The name "**Howland's**" would now take its place.

Although **H. G. Munger & Co.** traces its roots in Herkimer back to **1869**, occupying several different locations along North Main St., its final location was at **142 – 146 North Main St.**, built in **1918**, where it met its demise in **1970**.

As mentioned in the previous chapter, in **1968**, Genung's Inc. was bought out by a holding company called **Supermarkets General** (later becoming **Pathmark**). Part of the acquisition was **Howland's** department store chain based in Bridgeport, CT, then owned by Genung's Inc.

In **1970**, Supermarkets General combined **Genung's** and **Howland'**s, operating both under the "**Howland's**" name.

The first newspaper ad in **The Evening Telegram**, Herkimer, NY, listing the store as "**Howland's**" appeared in their **Sept. 14, 1970**, edition. This ad referred to Howland's as "**Formerly Munger's Now a Howland store.**"

Throughout the remainder of the year **1970**, Howland's ads would always refer to the fact that Munger's had previously occupied the building. One such reference was "**The New name for Your Friendly Munger's Store.**"

The first ad in **The Evening Telegram** listing only the "**Howland's**" name without a reference to "**Munger's**" appeared in their **January 1,1971** edition.

On **December 27, 1976**, at 5:30 p.m., the doors to the Munger's building were locked. The Howland's store moved out, re-opening at the Riverside Mall in Utica, leaving the old Munger's building vacant for the first time since the building was constructed in **1918**.

The headline of an article written by **Robert Pryor** in **The Evening Telegram**, Herkimer, NY, **December 26, 1976**, read in part, *Munger's Closes Tomorrow; Long Herkimer Tradition Dies – the last of the valley giants in retail business fades tomorrow – like the Empress Eugenie hat.*

Howland's store, which will close tomorrow forever, during the last week saw more than one woman with a tear in her eye. Howland's was its name, but in the minds of generations of Mohawk Valley people, it was still Munger's – an emporium of taste, elegance, and just the right item.

There were the J. B. Wells and Robert Fraser department stores in Utica, and then there was H. G. Munger & Co., which was cited in 1955 as one of the outstanding stores in America, in a small town or city.

Munger's once made those Empress Eugenie hats in its millinery department which had 24 women fashioning the latest creations. Munger's also custom-made dresses, sold silverware and jewelry, had rack after rack of fur coats and jackets, and thousands of other things.

On Christmas Eve, the remnants of a "Going Out of Business" sale strewn about the single floor that was still open. Merril Spanfelnor, who has shopped "Munger's" for many years, said sadly, "This is a crime to see this nice store gone."

When longtime manager Frederick Zeitler turns the key in the lock at 5:30 p.m. tomorrow, he will be shutting off 107 years of merchandising. Retail titan Henry G. Munger and a partner, Charles Avery, started the store when they came to Herkimer in 1869 and bought out a dry goods business.

All that will be left of Munger's are two oil portraits, one of old-time merchant Munger, and the other, of Henry M. Simmons, a grandson who modernized the store before his death in an automobile accident in 1938. The portraits, according to Zeitler, will go to the Herkimer County Historical Society this week, along with packages of memorabilia and newspaper advertising sheets that advertise things like wool delaines, merinos, serge's, hoop skirts, bustled, crinolines and mini-shirts.

Munger's not only played a role in the life of the community by offering goods, but also was a major employer.

The late Mrs. Elizabeth Burns, who was employed there 53 years, recalled in an interview that in 1955 there were 125 employees. And their record of longevity was exceptional. An employee with 30 years of service was average.

Downtown Herkimer, long a shopping magnet, has now lost two department stores within the past year with W. T. Grant Co. folding earlier.

The Howland employees still here are being transferred to the Howland store in Riverside Mall and the New Hartford Shopping Center.

And there was an unconfirmed report yesterday that negotiations for the sale of the Howland's building (actually three attached buildings) are still going on. It could not be learned what business it would house.

Following the closing of Holland's department store, the old Munger's building **stood vacant** for several years, until **1978**.

Munger's Closes Tomorrow; Long Herkimer Tradition Dies

In 1943 "Mungers" had a refined outside appearance.

Headline and Picture accompanying preceding transcribed article.

The Evening Telegram
Herkimer, NY
December 26, 1976
[Resized from Original]

CHAPTER TWENTY
WHO RAN THE STORE
[The Managers, Buyers and Associates who Made H. G. Munger & Co. Successful]

SUCCESSION OF MUNGER'S STORE MANAGEMENT – DOWNTOWN HERKIMER, NY STORE

Henry Gillette Munger:
Founder, President & Manager.
Served from **May 1869 – February 1928**.

Henry G. Munger retired in **Feb. 1928** when **American Department Stores** purchased **Munger's**. His grandson, **Henry Munger Simmons,** was then made store manager. **H. G. Munger** retired but was kept in an **advisory position** with the firm. **H. G. Munger** died on **July 14, 1933**.

Edgar Long Jackson:
Vice President of Munger's.
Served from **April 1899** – his death on **Dec. 12, 1939**.

In **April** of **1899**, E. L. Jackson, a long-time associate of Munger's, in charge at the time of the **Cloak Dept**. and **Head** of **Advertising**, purchased an interest in the Munger's store, thus becoming the first **vice president** of the newly formed firm of **H. G. Munger & Co.** **E. L. Jackson** died on **Dec. 12, 1939**.

Henry Munger Simmons:
Grandson of H. G. Munger.
Served as **Munger's Store Manager** from **February 1928** – his death on **Dec. 16, 1938**.

In **1922**, after graduating from **Yale University**, **H. G. Simmons** went to work in the **Advertising Department** of Munger's. Later he was promoted to **Advertising Director**. Upon word of **H. M. Simmons death**, **Henry J. Munger**, a cousin and officer in the company, arrived in Herkimer from his home in East Orange, NJ to assess the situation.

Leon V. Harris
Munger's Store Manager.
Served from **Dec. 1938 – Nov. 1, 1961**.

Leon started working at **Munger's** in **1905**, when he was **15** years old. Upon H. M. Simmons' death, Leon was appointed **store manager**. Leon retired on **Nov. 1, 1961**, following **Genung's Inc.** purchase of **Munger's**. Leon V. Harris died on **Oct. 16, 1978**.

Robert D. Caskey:
Munger's Store Manager.
Served from **November 1961 – September 1970.**

Robert was a part of the **Genung** management team when they purchased **Munger's**. **Robert D. Caskey** died on **March 12, 2014**.

Frederick H. Zeitler:
Howland's Store Manager.
Served from **Sept. 1970 – 1976.**

In **Sept. 1970, Munger's** (Genung's) was purchased by **Howland's**, a department store chain. The name "**Munger's**" came down and "**Howland's**" went up. **Munger's was no more.** Frederick managed the store until **1976**, when the store moved to **Riverside Mall** in **North Utica, NY**. **Frederick Harry Zeitler** died **June 21, 1997**.

Newell E. Adams:
Howland's Assistant Manager:
Served in this capacity during the **1970's.**

In the early **1970's,** Newell, who was working for **Montgomery Ward** in Herkimer at the time, was hired by **Howland's** store manager, **Fred Zeitler**, as Howland's new **assistant manager**. Later, Newell was reassigned to Holland's **New Hartford** store (previously Munger's) where he took on the duties of **Men's Wear Dept. Manager.** In **1976,** when the Herkimer store closed and relocated to **Riverside Mall** in North Utica, Newell was transferred to the new store, keeping his position as manager of their **Men's Wear Department. Newell E. Adams** died on **February 20, 1995**.

MUNGER'S EMPLOYEES

Over the years that the **H. G. Munger & Co**, Herkimer store was in operation, hundreds of individuals were employed, in various positions, at different times, throughout the store.

It is impossible to reconstruct a list of names which includes every employee. However, below and on the following pages are the names I have found or have been provided to me.

The most complete list of employees working for **Munger's**, during any given period, was listed in the **October 26, 1945, The Evening Telegram**, Herkimer, NY article entitled "**Munger Employees Set for V-Bond Campaign**," previously referenced in **Chapter Fifteen**.

It was reported, in the article, that store manager **Leon Harris** had devised a contest, within his store, to sell **War Bonds**. He divided up his employees into **six different teams,** each with its own unique name and captain. The contest was centered around which team could sell the most **V-Bonds** to its customers in an allotted period. The members of the winning team were given extra vacation time with pay.

Listed below are the team names, Captains, and employees on each given team:

Atomic Aces – Captain, Herberta Hammond; Marion Partington, Donald Miner, Flora Draheim, Mary Facteau, Leon Harris, Julia Quattlebaum, Frances Hartigan, Dorothy Noonan, Frances Bridger, Ruth Crill, Ethel Ownes, Mary Watson, Mrs. Josephine Wagoner, Mrs. Flora Morris, Mrs. Ethel Elsayer and Henry Harrer.

Old Glories – Captain, Elizabeth Burns; William Bleau, Florence Partion, Mildred Cole, Margaret Schwartz, Marjorie Zeitler, Dorothy Kirby, Malvena McCracken, Olive Laird, Jeannie Martin, Nellie Lever, Marguerite Chelle, Fred Zaugg, Charles Payne, Earl Kirby and Bess Maguire.

Stars & Stripes – Captain, A. F. Magee; John Wood, Arthur Miller, Hart Siedel, Geraldine Gertenbach, Myrta Pratt, Helen Brownell, June Weise, Ben Pooler, Mable Wainman, Ethel Taylor, Gertrude Mang, Chaterine Farrel, John Crim, Geraldine Reese and Shirley Krick.

Atom Misers – Captain, Mary Jones: Kristine Zguris, William Denny, Gladys Bronson, Francis Perry, Eva Hodge, Ida Farber, Lola Laun, Margaret Whalen, Sarah Loucks, Reba Talcott, Fanny Cherry, Ida Johnson, Mrs. James Mooney, Wilbur Lee, Mary Foley and Hubert Isnecker.

Victory Crusades – Captain, Albert Champney; Mae Cramer, Winfred Denny, Lavern Champney, Earle Mackenzie, Margaret Murnane, Elizabeth Mattis, Doris Williams, Ralph Webb, B. O. Lee, Eva Allen, Adrain Finley, Paul Palow, Josephine Dominico, Ethylwyn Murray, Mae Tuttle and Herbert Kinney.

Super-forts – Captain, Martha Babcock; Helen VanValkenburg, Inez Smith, Georgette Walstrom, Ruth Kirby, D. A. Schwartz, Maude Haupt, Mary Sanders, Clara Olyer, Egbert Vickery, Mary Falk, Marjorie Muray, Charlotte Cassidey, Walter Drapalski, George Kirby, Lela Welch and Eileen Mulhern.

Below I have listed other Munger employees' names, which I have found in newspaper articles and obituaries, along with the year of the publication:

1873: Mr. Clark Bull, **1888:** John Kelly, clerk, **1891:** Charles Wolcott, a "Leading Clerk," **1892:** Miss Hattie LaDue, **1894;** Mr. J. S. Mathews, **1895;** S. T. Prentiss, **1902:** John G. Terry, **1904:** A. Williams, Buyer and Jerry Strayer, Buyer, **1906:** Miss Jessie Wainman and Fred Snell. **1910:** Miss Marion Pierce, **1911:** Miss Marcia Shoemaker, **1913:** E. K. LaDue, **1917:** Miss Freida (nee Harter) Vernon Clark, Clerk, **1925:** Miss Emma Clark, **1957:** Johann R. Heiman, worked in Upholstery Dept.

MUNGER'S DEPARTMENT BUYERS

Below is a list of **buyers** who purchased goods to sell in the **Munger's** store, in **1957**, the year of **Herkimer's Sesquicentennial.**

The list appeared in a **Munger's** advertisement in **The Evening Telegram, Herkimer, NY**, in their **Sesquicentennial edition** that year:

Mr. Lee, buyer **of FABRICS, LINENS, DOMESTICS & PATTERNS.**

Mrs. Zeitler, buyer of **NEEDLEWORK, SPORTSWEAR, NECKWEAR, HANDERCHIEFS, GIRLS' WEAR, INFANTS' WEAR & GIRL SCOUTS.**

Miss Crill, buyer of **TOILETRIES, LEATHER GOODS, UMBRELLAS, GLOVES & HOSIERY.**

Mr. Miner, buyer of **SILVERWARE & COSTUME JEWELRY**. In charge of **watch** and **jewelry repairs.**

Miss Talcott, buyer of **PIN MONEY DRESSES, HOUSE DRESSES & LINGERIE.**

Mrs. Hammond, Fashion coordinator, Bridal consultant and buyer of **BETTER DRESSES.**

Miss Chelle, buyer of **COATS & SUITS.**

Mr. Magee, buyer of **MEN'S FURNISHINGS, BOYS' WEAR, LUGGAGE & BOY SCOUT NEEDS.**

Mrs. Olyer, buyer of **CHINA** and **CRYSTAL, HOUSEWARES, NOTIONS, STATIONERY, CANDY, FOODS, GIFTWARES & LAMPS.**

Mr. Zeitler, buyer of **PAINT & TOOLS.**

Mr. Bleau, buyer of **FURNITURE, RUGS & TOYS.**

Mr. Webb, buyer of **WOMEN'S** and **CHILDREN'S SHOES.**

Mrs. Cole, buyer of **CORSETS.**

Miss Cunningham, buyer of **MILLENERY.**

Mrs. Jones, buyer of **draperies.**

Mr. John, buyer of **FURS**.

MUNGER'S FIRST WOMAN EMPLOYEE & BUYER

Miss Elfie Harter has the double distinction of being **H. G. Munger & Co.'s first woman employee** and **first women buyer**.

The Evening Telegram, Herkimer, NY, **June 25, 1940**, reported, ***Store Honors Retiring Employee for 55 Years*** *– Miss Elfie Harter, first woman clerk to be employed by any Herkimer store, was honored last night at a dinner given by H. G. Munger & Co., executives and employees at Three Islands, Newport. She is retiring in July after 55 years of service.*

More than 125 fellow workers and guests attended. Bruce Steele, grandson of the late H. G. Munger, founder of the store, was toastmaster. L. V. Harris, Manager, congratulated Miss Harter upon her long service and expressed regret at her retirement.

Entered Store at 18*: Miss Harter entered the employment of the store at 18 years of age. As the business expanded. Munger trained several of his employees as buyers. Miss Harter, among the five selected, was the first woman buyer in Central New York. She later became a department manager and during subsequent years, her responsibilities increased.*

The **October 5, 1945**, edition of **The Evening Telegram**, Herkimer NY, reported, ***Elfie Harter Observes 85th Birthday Date*** *– Miss Elfie Harter, who was the first woman to become an employee at the H. G. Munger Co., today was quietly celebrating her 85th birthday "just the same as any, old day" at her home, 429 Prospect St.*

Miss Harter first went to work in Munger's in 1884 a few years after she completed her schooling and was in charge of the notion, ribbon and hosiery department.

Open New Field *– At that time, this department was one of the most important in the store. There were no ready-made clothes, and housewives were required to make their own dresses, blouses, infant's garments.*

In this section of the store, they could find imported laces and embroideries for trimmings and various sewing aides. Miss Harter said that only ready-made black satin petticoats and the "Old Mother Hubbard" dresses could be purchased at the time.

Sometime later, one of the best dress makers was employed to make dresses, which were then sold. Miss Harter became the store's veteran employee when she retired after 56 years of work in 1940.

__Lifelong Resident__- She was born in the house in which she now resides on Oct. 5, 1860, a daughter of William and Margaret VanHorn Harter. All her education was received in local schools (the high school at that time was located on N. Washington St.).

A member of the Reformed Church, she is also affiliated with the Ladies' Aid and the Missionary Society and served as a Sunday School Teacher for 40 years. She was also a member of the choir for the same length of time.

Elfie A. Harter was born on **October 5, 1860**, in **Herkimer, NY**, a daughter of **Capt. William** (1818 – 1874) and **Margaret** (nee **Vanhorn**) **Harter** (1833 – 1913). Elfie's father was listed as a "**Farmer**" in the **1870 U.S. Federal Census**, count taken four years before his death.

William and **Margaret Harter** had **six** known children, according to the "**Familysearch.org**" website: Daisy Harter (1858 – Deceased), **Elfie A. Harter** (1860 – 1951), **Willie Harter** (1863 – Deceased), **Hamilton Harter** (1865 – Deceased), **William Hamilton Harter** (1866 – 1920) and **Anna Belle Harter** (1868 – 1943).

Anna Belle Harter, Elfie's sister, was a **music** and **piano teacher** by profession.

The **1900 U.S. Federal Census** lists Elfie as a "**Saleslady – Dry Goods**," 1910; "**Clerk – Dept. Store**," 1920; "**Saleslady – Retail Dry Goods**," 1930; "**Buyer – Dept. Store**." 1940; "**Buyer – Dept. Store**."

Elfie A. Harter died on **January 26, 1951**, at the age of **90 yrs**. She is buried at **Oak Hill Cemetery, Herkimer, NY.**

Elfie's small obituary appeared in the **January 27, 1951, The Evening Telegram, Herkimer, NY**, and states as follows, *__HARTER__ – Elfie, 90, of 429 Prospect St., in Memorial Hospital on Friday, Jan. 26, 1951. The funeral will be held at 2 p.m. Sunday at her late home with the Rev. J. Foster Welwood officiating. Interment in Oak Hill Cemetery. Friends may call her late home Saturday evening. Services directed by Alton J. Fenner.*

The **Evening Telegram, Herkimer, NY, May 4, 1955**, reported, in part, *__Munger's Employees Honor Two Retiring Veterans at Dinner__ – Over 100 persons from Munger's last night attended a* *dinner party at the Black Dalia, Poland, to honor Mrs. Bess Burns and William E. Denny on their retirement from the store after long business associations.*

Leon Harris, Manager of Munger's, was the principal speaker. He recalled his pleasant association with Mrs. Burns and Mr. Denny "as something I will long remember and cherish."

"They always had the interests of the store at heart," he said. "They both exemplified the highest standards of integrity and loyalty. I am sure they can both look back to the many years given to the store, with a feeling of great satisfaction in knowing the important part they played in the store's growth."

Bruce Steel, speaking on behalf of the Munger Holding Company, expressed the company's gratitude to Mrs. Burns and Mr. Denny for their long, faithful service. He presented Mrs. Burns with a diamond ring as a token of appreciation of her 53 years with Munger's.

Albert Scalise, who has been in charge of the tailor shop and who is leaving Munger's, was also honored and presented with a gift from his associates.

Mr. Denny who, like Mrs. Burns, had been a familiar figure at the store for many years and always wore a red rose in his buttonhole, was presented with a special rose in commemoration of the occasion.

William Edward Denny (1873 – 1956) was listed in the **1940 U.S. Federal Census** as a "**Superintendent – Clothing Store.**" He is also mentioned in an article in **The Glen Falls Times, Nov. 14, 1945**, referring to him as "**Superintendent of the H. G. Munger & Co.**" His obituary states that in **1934**, William moved from **Glen Falls, NY**, where he was the **Shoe Department Manager** for the **F. W. Wiley** store, to Herkimer, NY, to work at the **H. G. Munger & Co.** store. He was married to **Caroline M.** (nee **Littlejohn**) **Denny** (1886 -1945). They are both buried at **Mount Hope Cemetery, Norwich, NY.**

Several Munger's Store Clerk's 1940's
From the Files of the Herkimer Co.
Historical Society, Herkimer, NY
[Resized from Original]
Front row, L. to R., Bertha Hewes, Mary Jones, ?, Frances Hartigan, Flora Morris ?, Clara Olyer, Marjorie Zeitler.
Back row, L to R., Mary Facteau, Mary Falk, ?, Eva Allen, Bess Burns, Ruth Crill, ?, Georgetta Barnes Walstrom.

Sales Personnel Of Munger's): Pictured are the sales personnel of the store in 1948. From left to right are (first row): Kathleen Bell, Bess Maguire, Margaret Schwartz, Delores Tarm, Mary Casler, Ethelwyn Murray, ? Nancarrow, and Helen Van Valkenburg. (second row): Mabel Wainman, Frances Bridger, Helen Miller, Beautrice Burny, Robert Dingman, Helen Brownell, Appolonia Nedzynski, and Nora Lally. (Courtesy of Mary Falk).

1948

Around table from left to right
1 Herberta Hammond
2 Josephine Christiano
3 Vera Jones
4 Ida Happich
5 Maggie Schwarty
6 Betty Mat..
7 Irtha Heuer
8 Francis Jordan
9 me
10 Jeanne Perry
11 Margaret Blause
12 Mary Picteau

Standing front to R
1 Mary Acke
2 Hilda Picknik
3 Margaret Nancarrol
4 Sadie Perry
5 Fannie Chesky
6 Mrs. Illene
7 Josephine Mohimero

March 3, 1948

Farewell Party for
Herberta Hammond
at Chirico's

Fairwell Party for Munger's Employee
Herberta Hammond at Chirico's
March 3, 1948
From the Files of the Herkimer Co.
Historical Society, Herkimer, NY
[Resized from Original]

Munger's Women's Day
March 14, 1952
Bertha Hewes
Mary Jones
Barbara Keene
Frances Hartigan
Flora Morris
Clara Oleyer
Mary Zeitler
(Me) Mary Facteau
Mary Falk
Eleanor Cook
Eva Allen
Bess Burns
Ruth Gill
Rtha Talcott
Georgie Walstrom

Women's Day at Mungers
March 14, 1952
From the files of the Herkimer Co.
Historical Society, Herkimer, NY
[Resized from Original]

MUNGER'S "WOMEN'S DAY"—Women of the H. G. Munger & Co. store, Herkimer, assumed active management of the store yesterday during the annual "Woman's Day." Male employes dressed as women were around the store. Following lunch in the Prospect Hotel the men stopped for this picture. They are, from the left, seated, James Jackson, Fred Zeitler, Winfield Denny, Leon Harris, general manager. Standing, Benjamin Pooler, Donald Miner, John O'Brien, William Bleau, Lee Happe, Frank Lichtarski, Alfred Hallstrom, John Wood and Burt O. Lee.

From the Files of the Herkimer Co.
Historical Society, Herkimer, NY
[Resized from Original]

MUNGER'S EMPLOYEES — Most of the employees of the former H.G. Munger Department Store, one of the finer stores of its time in Upstate New York, were members of the Poulie - Poulie Club and convened frequently to dine, this at the Prospect Hotel during its early days. Photo was contributed by H. Paul Draheim.

Delila Allen
Olive Reid
Lorene Champney
Gladys Bronson
Bess O'ryan
Flora Vom Vatel Draheim
Marguerite Chilli
Georgette Bauer

Mildred Cole
Florence Partlow
Frances Hartigan
Kay Long
Ruth Allen
Bertha Lewis
Marjory Pettis

The Way It Was

MUNGERS EMPLOYEES — Munger's Department Store of Herkimer held a Christmas party at the Hotel Utica in 1941 when this picture was taken. The photo was contributed by Alton Robinson of Mohawk whose mother worked at the store.

Evening Telegram, Herkimer, NY
May 31, 1985
From the Files of the Herkimer Co.
Historical Society, Herkimer, NY
[Resized from Original]

CHAPTER TWENTY-ONE
NEW LIFE FOR AN OLD BUILDING
[The Bonnie's Arts & Crafts Years]

In **1978**, two years after Holland's closed, **Frederic J. "Fred" King**, who ran the **King Craft Company**, a wholesale arts and crafts business, purchased the old Munger's building on North Main St. in Herkimer, moving his business into the top two floors of the building.

That same year, his wife, **Bonnie**, who ran **Bonnie's Arts & Crafts** store on Green Street in Herkimer, moved into the right side of the old Munger's building, where **Wakefield Furniture** is located today.

The **1977 Herkimer Business Directory** lists **Bonnie's Arts & Crafts** as located at **117 Green St.** in Herkimer. The **1978 Directory** lists the address as **140 N. Main Street** (the old Munger's building).

In conjunction with his wholesale operation, Fred ran **King's Court Mall** on the first floor of the building. The Court consisted of various businesses which rented space from him. Over the years, the mall was home to a pet store, a gift shop, barber shop, newsstand, jeweler, office supply store and a flooring store in King's Court.

At one point, in the **mid 1980's, Dr. Ralph Slayon** headed a local theater group, **Theater for Young People in Herkimer Co.**, based in the **King's Court Theater**, located in the Munger's building's lower level, in the rear of the building. The theater was referred to as a "**block box area theater**." The term "black box" refers to the black walls of the theater, and "area" refers to the fact that the audience surrounds the actors while they perform.

Frederic J. "Fred" King died on **October 23, 1998**, and is buried at **Millers Mills Cemetery**, Millers Mills, Herkimer Co., NY.

Eventually, Fred's two sons, **Gary** and **Steve**, would become involved in operating **King's Crafts** until its closing in **2018**.

Gary King remembers the old "**Chat and Chew**" dinner, owned by **Gordon & Sharon Turner**, which occupied the space where the **Munger's Shoe Store** was once located.

Fred's widow, **Bonnie June** (nee **Young**) **King** would continue to operate **Bonnie's Arts & Crafts**, retiring in the early **2000s**, after **twenty-five years** in business.

Bonnie June King died on **March 30, 2014**, and is buried beside her husband at **Millers Mills Cemetery.**

Following the closing of **Bonnie's Arts & Crafts** in the early **2000s**, several businesses came and went in the old Munger's building. One that came to mind was **Oats Gym**.

CHAPTER TWENTY-TWO
THE H. G. MUNGER'S BUILDING: LOOKING AHEAD
[Joseph Chilelli Purchases the Old Munger's Building]

In **September 2018**, local realtor and businessman **Joseph Chilelli** purchased the **H. G. Munger** building in downtown Herkimer, NY, with the idea of helping to revitalize Herkimer's downtown shopping area on North Main Street.

Chilelli, a former **Long Island, NY** native, moved his family to Herkimer in **1999**. He stated in his professional bio. that *I fell in love with the Mohawk Valley not only for its beauty and abundant natural resources, but also for the kindness and generosity of its people.*

I have been involved in real estate for many years, selling all types of properties and everything in between. I am very much involved and well-known in the community, from being a former County Legislator to helping initiate St. Anthony's Festival on South Main Street in Herkimer. I am very much involved not only with my local Church, but also with many of the activities in the area. In my spare time, I enjoy tending my own vineyard and fruit orchard and look forward to making my own wine each year.

Shortly after Chilelli purchased the Munger building at 142 N. Main Street in Herkimer, a partial renovation took place. **Renewed and Rescued**, a "quality" consignment antique shop owned by Tammy Crossway, was the first store to move in under the building 's banner of "**Mohawk Valley Community Market – Antiques & More.**" On **July 1, 2021, the first anniversary** of the **Mohawk Valley Community Market** was celebrated.

Tammy's shop recently celebrated its **fifth** anniversary.

As you enter the Munger's building, you will be greeted by **Renewed and Rescued's** friendly staff. Beyond their space, on the first floor, are assorted antiques and collectibles sold on consignment by individual vendors.

On **Friday, September 2, 2022**, the **lower level** was **opened**. Much of this area is used by consignment dealers. Chilelli and his wife, Ninfa, also operate a high-quality **jewelry counter** on the lower level as well as an **Italian Market**.

On **Saturday, August 5, 2023**, the Chilelli's opened **Munger's 1918 Luncheonette** on the lower level of the Munger's building. Here is where shoppers can take a break and enjoy a delicious cup of coffee with homemade pastries or heartwarming soup, among other delicious foods.

Directly to and adjoining the right side of Munger's main building is **Wakefield Furniture**, its address being **138 N. Main St.**

For years, **W. T. Grant** occupied this space with the remnants of the **Deimel & Schermer's Grand Opera House** on the top floor of the building, which had closed years ago.

Wakefield Furniture is a family-owned **furniture** and **mattress store**, managed by **John W. Wakefield**. He has managed the store from **January 2019** to the present.

On special occasions, Chilelli has conducted guided tours through the old Munger's building, with an emphasis on the building's rich history and that of the **H. G. Munger & Co.**, once the **Mercantile Palace** of Herkimer Co., NY.

Chilelli has also set up a small but growing **H. G. Munger & Co. Museum** on the lower level of the Munger's building, close in proximity to the **Munger's 1918 Luncheonette**.

The next big project, connected with the Munger's building, is that of bringing the old **passenger elevator** back to working condition so that easy access to all floors can become a reality, and the upper two floors of the building can be utilized.

Munger's 1918 Luncheonette
Lower Level
Mohawk Valley Community Market
142 N. Main St., Herkimer, NY

Munger's 1918 Luncheonette
Lower Level
Mohawk Valley Community Market
142 N. Main St., Herkimer, NY

The H. G. Munger's Museum
Lower Level
The Mohawk Community Market
142 N. Main St., Herkimer, NY

The H. G. Munger's Museum
The museum can be viewed during normal business hours
in the lower level of the
Mohawk Valley Community Market
142 N. Main Street, Herkimer, NY

CHAPTER TWENTY-THREE
A TIME FOR REMINISCING
[Past H. G. Munger & Co. Employees Tell Their Stories]

On **Wednesday** evening, **January 11, 2024**, from **5pm to 7pm**, a gathering of past **H. G. Munger & Co.** employees met at the **Munger's 1918 Luncheonette, 142 N. Main St. in Herkimer**, located in the basement of the old **Munger's** building, to reminisce of days gone by.

The following is a list of the former employees in attendance:

1. Cathy Blackwell: Cathy worked in the **Munger's Beauty Shop** (**second floor** next to the **Lingerie Dept**.) starting in **1967** as a **beautician** and **hair stylist**. This was her first job after graduating from the **Utica School of Beauty Culture** in **1966**. Her supervisor at Munger's was **Anna Fiedel**.

When Cathy was hired, there was already a "**Cathy**" working in the Beauty Shop by the name of **Cathy Carpenter**. Thus, to avoid confusion, when customers booked their appointments, **Cathy Blackwell** was given the name "**Sue.**"

The **Beauty Shop** consisted of **six stations** or separate **booths** to service customers.

Another beautician who Cathy (Sue) remembers working with was **Toni** (nee **Sanganetti**) **Heimer**.

Cathy also had a friend, **Jackie Shaul**, who worked in the **Jewelry Department**.

Cathy Blackwell left **Munger's** in **1969**.

2. Sharon (nee **Lynch**) **Yeager**: Sharon worked in the **Munger's Lingerie Department**, located on the **second floor**, from **October** thru **December 1967**, during the **Christmas** season.

Sharon doesn't remember her **supervisor's** name, only that she spoke with an **English** accent.

The boxes of lingerie were on shelves behind the counter. When a customer asked to see a particular piece, Sharon was trained to take **three separate boxes** from the shelf: low grade, moderately priced, and top of the line. She would place them on the counter for the customer to see. Of course she would always start her **sales pitch** by showing the customer the "**top of the line**" first.

3. Tom Adams: Tom worked at **Munger's** during his **junior** and **senior year** in high school, **1967 – 1969**, in the **shoe department**.

The **shoe department** was a "**leased**" department, not owned by **Munger's**. It had its own entrance through a door on the **far-left** front side of **Munger's** building. It was basically a **store within a store**.

Tom's brother **Tim** would later work at the store. Tom's father, **Newell Adams,** was Munger's **assistant store manager** at the time.

4. Tim Adams: Tim worked in the old **Munger's** building when it went by the name of "**Holland's**." He was employed from **1971** until the store's closing in **1976**, when the store relocated to the **Riverside Mall** in Utica.

During his time with **Holland's,** Tim worked as a **passenger elevator Operator**, a **shoe department salesman**, and an employee in the **Receiving** area of the store.

Tim remembers that a "**Store Directory**" hung on one of the walls of the elevator, listing each **department** and **what floor it was located on**. He also remembers that a woman by the name of "**Ida**" managed the **shoe department**.

Tim said that he thought the **Munger's shoe department** had exclusive rights to the selling of the **Daniel Green** line of shoes in the area, which were manufactured in nearby **Dolgeville, NY** by the **Daniel Green Company**.

One story which Tim delights in telling concerns his tenure as a Holland's **passenger elevator operator**.

Prefix: As one approaches the store's passenger elevator, with entrances on the lower level, main floor and top two floors, they are greeted by an ornate pair of glass enclosed wooden framed doors. Once opened, an expandable scissor gate, which the operator could open and shut, secured the actual elevator cage.

The operator could not only cause the elevator to stop on any given floor but could also, if desired, have the elevator stop between floors. When in operation, the passengers could look straight beyond the scissor gate, viewing the front walls of the elevator shaft as the elevator was raised or lowered.

One day, as Tim tells it, *With no passengers aboard and a bit of mischief on my mind, I decided to stop the elevator between floors and with a black magic marker, I wrote the following on the shaft wall in front of me*: "**May all your ups and downs be between the sheets.**" *I thought it was a neat idea at the time.*

*Around closing time that same day, as I was bringing store manager Fred Zeitler down from the third floor to the main floor, my newly drawn graffiti caught Mr. Zeitler's eye. "**Did you do that?**" asked Mr. Zeitler. I admitted that the artwork was mine.*

When the elevator came to a rest on the main floor, "Wait here!" he ordered. "I'll be right back." When Mr. Zeitler returned, he was carrying a bucket of paint and a paint roller, both of which he **handed to me.** *"Here, stay as late as you must but I want the entire shaft wall facing away from the elevator freshly painted from top floor to bottom." This I begrudgingly did.*

I can now boast that I was the very last person to have ever painted the entire old Munger's passenger elevator shaft.

Another story which Tim tells concerns a certain female employee (name not remembered) who also worked a shift as the passenger elevator operator.

She was pleasant enough but was plagued with poor hygiene when it came to body odor.

Over time, the passengers/customers, having to endure sharing the small, enclosed elevator space with her, and thus, the unpleasant odor, had had enough and finally reported the situation to the top management.

Store manager **Fred Zeitler** passed on the responsibility of dealing with the problem to his assistant manager, my father, **Newell Adams**.

One day Newell sat the woman down and delicately confronted her with the customers' concerns, suggesting that she try **using a bit of deodorant** before coming to work.

Following this meeting, there were no more complaints concerning the matter.

As Tim might say, "**There were a lot of ups and downs being an elevator operator during the 1970's.**"

5. Sharon (nee **Lynch**) **Yeage**r: Sharon worked in **Munger's Lingerie Department**, on the second floor, as **Christmas** help, from **October** thru **December 1967**.

———————

A former employee unable to attend:

1. **Kay** (nee **McEzoy**) **Engle**: Kay was born and raised in **Little Falls, NY**. During high school she worked evenings at the local **Woolworth's 5 & 10** in Little Falls.

In **1945** Kay graduated from **Little Falls High School**.

Following graduation, unsure of what to do next in life, she found employment with the **Charles Hansen Laboratories** in Little Falls, a company which made "**junket**" tablets used in the manufacturing of commercial cheese.

At the age of nineteen, a year later, in **July** of **1947**, she started working for **Munger's** Department Store in Herkimer.

During the week, she would take the bus from Little Falls into Herkimer to work. On Friday's, working the evening shift, she would take the train.

Her first job at Munger's was in their "**lending library**" located in the left rear of the store on the main floor. The library acted much like a regular library where one could check out a book and return it later once read. Being the only clerk in that area of the store, she felt isolated with not much to do. She eventually requested and received a transfer to a different department.

Her new assignment was at the "**Customer Service**" counter on the main floor where she would **wrap gifts** for customers, assist in "**Lost and Found**," and **direct customers** to their desired department(s) throughout the store.

Besides herself, one other girl, who Kay befriended, worked at the customer service desk along with Kay.

A part of her job, at the customer service desk, was that of making change for customers in nearby departments. Kay remembers that when change was needed, a clerk would tap his/her scissors on their respective counter to get her attention.

Kay thoroughly enjoyed working at the "**customer service" counter**, where she wasn't tied down to one isolated spot in the store as she had been in the lending library.

Kay remembers that she enjoyed eating her sack lunch, which she brought from home, on the glamourous **balcony** overlooking the main sales floor. She remembers a piano was located on the balcony but doesn't remember it ever being played. At the present time, this piano still exists and is just located behind the balcony.

In **July** of **1947**, Kay left Munger's and started attending the **State Teachers' College** in **Oswego**,

NY.

Throughout her life, "teaching" was Kay's main career. Toward the end of her working days, she worked in the **advertising department** of the local newspaper in **Poughkeepsie, NY.**

"All in all," Kay said, **"I really enjoyed working at Munger's, if only for a short while."**

Author's Notes:

The following article appeared in **The Evening Telegram, Herkimer, NY, February 6, 1946**. In part here is how it read, ***Munger's Adds Loan Library*** *– A new circulating library has been added to the recently opened Book Shop in the H. G. Munger Co. basement for booklovers of Herkimer and adjoining towns and villages, it was announced today.*

Plans are underway to make this new library up to date in every way, and it was said that ample numbers of copies of the latest books will be on hand as soon as a book is published.

In order to take care of the widest reading preference, the shelves will include volumes dealing with mystery, adventure and romance in both fiction and non-fiction types.

This new department, together with the Book Shop, opened shortly before Christmas, will be located in the basement until the additional floor is completed. Both will then be moved to the main floor.

Those non-former employees in attendance:

1. Joseph Chilelli: Owner of the **H. G. Munger & Co**. building and **Operator** of the **Munger's 1918 Luncheonette** as well as The **Italian Market. Also manages** the vendors located on the Basement Floor.

2. Ninfa Chilelli: Joseph's wife, who assists her husband in various capacities, including cooking, baking, etc.

3. Tom Johnson: Author and **Researcher** of his upcoming book on the history of **H. G. Munger & Co.**

4. Mary Johnson: Tom's wife, who is assisting him with proofreading and editing.

5. Melanie Lopata: Author and **Owner** of **Get it Write Publishing**.

———————

A few weeks after the **"Former Munger Employees"** gathering, I was visiting the lower level of the **Mohawk Valley Community Market** when I noticed a woman admiring the **H. G. Munger**

Museum, located not far from the **Munger's 1918 Luncheonette**.

The small museum consists of vintage Munger's advertisements, photographs, letters, postcards, store blueprints and other memorabilia from the store's past.

I introduced myself, and then the woman introduced herself to me as **Laura Hailston**.

I told her that I was currently researching and writing a book on the history of **H. G. Munger & Co**. and its department store.

She then replied to me, "**Well, I've never worked for Munger's, but I have a great true story for your book**."

Judy Steele used to work for the Light Department in Ilion and her husband, Ray, I believe was Town Supervisor in German Flats. Judy was a wonderful woman with a wonderful sense of humor.

Judy told me this story many times and I would always get a chuckle out of it.

I think she and her husband were planning a trip to Vegas.

She was a matron at this time; she wasn't a young woman.

She went to Munger's to buy some lingerie. She wanted the most expensive lingerie that Munger's had so she went to the Lingerie Dept. Back in the day, you always had to be waited on.

Thus, the woman who worked the counter went in back and brought out some lingerie. So Judy's looking at it. She's holding it up and then she asks the woman, "Do you have any more?"

The woman (clerk) is very accommodating. She's looking under the counter and finds different styles to bring out.

Judy always dressed in style, everything matched, everything put together well.

The woman that worked the counter was very curious. "Is this a wedding gift for the bride?"

Judy replied, "Oh no, no!"

The woman is still very curious. "May I ask what's this for?"

Judy, who is very determined and set in her ways, said, "Oh, it's for me."

"My husband and I are going to take a trip. We're flying and I'm going to be wearing this and I

want everyone to know that when the plane crashes, I want to be identified as the woman wearing the most expensive lingerie that Munger's in Herkimer has to offer!"

That was Judy!

WALKING DOWN
MUNGER'S MEMORY LANE

By Thomas Lee Johnson

Did You Know
A mercantile palace once graced our Herkimer town.
It was located on Main Street in its bustling downtown.
Those who worked and shopped there alike, knew it by name and knew it by sight.

Back in the day, it was off to Munger's you'd go
to purchase your dry goods, men and women with children in tow.

The brightly decorated front windows greeted you
as you came from the sidewalk into the store.
And once inside, glass fronted wooden display cases would line your way
for a perfect shopping experience, what else is there to say.

An old-time elevator and its operator would take you from floor to floor.
A salesperson waited on you and would write up your sale.
A pneumatic tube would bring you your change.
And as for selection there was always something from
pin money to expensive in your price range.

There was even an orchestra which once played on the balcony overlooking the main floor.
What an elegant atmosphere—who could ask for more.

And each year, as the seasons they changed, so did Munger's décor,
which took you from summer to fall to winter to spring
inside of their modern up-to-date store.

Memories now are all we have left
of those times so very long ago,
when a mercantile palace called Munger's
was definitely the must place to go.

CHAPTER TWENTY-FOUR
MY LITTLE COLONEL SHIRLEY TEMPLE DOLL
[Another Memory From a former Employee of the H. G. Munger & Co.]

Although she was unable to attend the Munger's Get Together, **Donna Clark Veeder**, age 90, a former **Munger's** employee, was represented via a donation and a written story which she had given to the current Munger store owner, **Joseph Chilelli** on **September 16, 2023**.

Both Donna's donation and her written story are on display in the small **H. G. Munger Museum**, which Chilelli has assembled on the lower level of the building near his **Munger's 1918 Luncheonette**.

The following is a transcription of Donna's letter:

"The Little Colonel": Shirley Temple Doll

I came to Munger's to work in the Christmas season of 1959. My husband Nick and I had moved to Little Falls the year before, but during the spring of '59, we found a farm near Van Hornesville, NY, moving there in the fall. I started work at Munger's about mid-November in their Drapery Department. Nick drove me to work and picked me up. I did not drive. My boss was Mrs. Jones; her second in command was Mrs. Smith. I hope I have their names in proper order!

I had an art degree but knew nothing of how to sell or make draperies. I learned. These two ladies were only too happy to teach me what I needed to know. Don't know how I did it because it entails math, my worst subject. I used a method of measuring, combining some math and some Eyeing it! (I have an internal mental measuring system that must have been honed by the artwork). The repeat patterns of materials helped. Mrs. Jones or Mrs. Smith always checked my measurements and figures. Sometimes both did! Good thing!

The Drapery Department was attached to the Upholstery Department. Materials were carried for curtains, draperies and furniture. Johnny Heimann was the Master Upholsterer. I would deliver materials back to his work room. I liked to watch him work, having always been interested in the process. Upholstery is something like making sculpture. He could draw patterns, cut and bend and sew and tack that material in place as if it had grown on the chairs. I still have one he covered here at home. His fellow worker was Hans. I do not remember Hans' last name. It was seldom used. He spoke little English, mumbled a lot in German and when he walked by any of us females in the department, he exclaimed, under his breath, "Vimen!!! (Women!!!).

Both had graduated from technical schools in Germany. They were Masters of their trade. Hans did refinishing. I remember once that a beautiful dining table came in with a large, ugly scratch on the surface at one end. It was Hans' job to fix that. He used shellac, I think, very fine sandpapers and a personally handmade pumice buffer, working for many weeks. Once done, you could never have seen that scratch! He could accomplish furniture magic! Both of them could.

The other department attached to draperies was in a room further back in a corner: Drapery Alterations. Two ladies worked there making alterations for window treatments. They also had the job of pressing all curtains and draperies to be ready for customers, shortening or lengthening curtains so beautifully that you could not tell anything had been done to them. Watching them work taught me a lot! Later, using knowledge gained there, I made my own draperies for our farm home. And once, I slip-covered a large couch using memory and some How-to-pamphlets found at the Herkimer Co. Home Bureau. All those materials were bought at Munger's Drapery Department, of course. I met all these Fine Craftsmen and Women at Munger's.

Sometimes I worked with the man who decorated the large front windows. He created display areas in all departments. He was Mr. Campbell. (That came to me out of the blue last night!) He had made all the Christmas Street decorations for the Village of Herkimer for years. I remember cut-out reindeer and angels. I liked to watch him work when he came to our department.

A few times when we were slack with work to do, I was given the job of following him around to be his Go-for. Once he asked me to go up in the attic of the building to find something for him, telling me where to look. The place turned out to be an old empty theater! It was very dark and very hot. Large open cardboard boxes were lined up across the balconies far as I could see. Box after box lay in the empty spaces left where seats had once stood. I found the row where I was to look. I had not brought a flashlight so resorted to feeling inside boxes for whatever it was I was seeking. All of a sudden, there was something furry!

"Oh dear! I hope this is not a rat!"

It didn't bite. Feeling further, lo and behold, it was a large doll! I pulled her out to find her still in her original costume. She was a Shirley Temple, blonde curls, flirty brown eyes, open mouth, tiny teeth and all, dressed as "The Little Colonel!" (I've since seen the movie on Turner Classics.) Her cape was cobalt blue velvet with a red satin lining, round white collar and red tie. She wore a white satin dress with long sleeves, long white stockings, plus all her original underwear and her little white leatherette shoes, snapped at the instep. She was the last thing in the world I had ever thought to find in that old box! Had she lain there since the 1930's? I did not find the item Mr. Campbell wanted, but told him of finding the doll. He said, "Oh, take it home with you! No one will mind."

So I did! I've kept her safe all these years in my doll collection. Now, I am returning her to her original home. She is a Counter-Top Display Baby Doll, 16" high. Unmarked. She is mostly composition: body, arms and hands, socket head and lower legs. Upper legs are cloth. She needs a stand which we never found.

   This Shirley was an original model made for the movie, "The Little Colonel" of 1933, the year I was born! I had wanted a Shirley Temple Doll most of my young life. We never could afford one. She was a very special gift! I hope others will enjoy her presence here, back in her original home at Munger's Department Store

Donna Clark Veeder, Age 90: 9/16/23

1933 Shirley Temple Doll

CHAPTER TWENTY-FIVE

BONUS CHAPTER
DEIMEL & SCHERMER'S
GRAND OPERA HOUSE
[138 – 140 North Main Street, Herkimer, NY]
1887 – 1917

No history of **H. G. Munger & Co.**, its store and building, would be complete without referring to the **Grand Opera House**, in Herkimer. Over the years, since **1918**, **Munger's** and the **Grand Opera House** have become **synonymous**.

It has been said that from the end of the **Civil War** through the **1920's** opera houses throughout the country were central to the American Way of Life.

Local opera houses, however, were generally not used for "**operas**" as one might think of the opera houses of Europe. Rather, they were home to a variety of entertainments, **operas** notwithstanding, including community **dances**, **orchestra** and **band** performances, **high school graduations**, **conventions**, and other **civic functions** as well as **traveling theatrical companies** and **vaudeville troops.**

They were a part of the fabric of each community in which they resided and were used for anything and everything that a large indoor space could provide for. They were the **auditoriums** and **event centers** of yesterday.

The term "**opera house**" was, thus, a misnomer which was used to appease those, religious and otherwise, who thought the "**theater**" was a **sinful** or **wicked** place. By referring to the theater as an "**opera house**," the hall took on an **air of refinement** and, thus, was accepted by all persuasions of the public.

During the latter part of the eighteen hundreds, opera houses were nothing new to the Herkimer area.

There was the **Fox Opera House**, operated by **Charles J. Fox**, who had built the **Fox Block** on North Main Street in **Herkimer**, around **1864**. Fox also, at one time, had owned and operated the **Waverly Hotel** to the right of his Fox Block.

In **1870**, two opera houses opened locally: **Varley House**, in **Mohawk,** proprietor **Thomas**

Varley (1817 – 1877); and **Maben's Opera House** in **Ilion**, built by **Dr. H. B. Maben**.

On **Tuesday evening, October 7, 1884, Deimel & Schermer's Grand Opera House** opened in downtown **Herkimer**.

The event, which opened the **Grand Opera House** that evening, was the presentation of the opera "**Bohemian Girl**," starring **Emma Abbott**.

Emma Abbott (1850 – 1891) was an American operatic Soprano and impresario, best known for possessing a powerfully pure, clear voice of resonance.

The **Herkimer Democrat, dated October 1, 1884,** stated *Deimel & Schermer's New Opera House will be opened on the evening of October 7th, by the Emma Abbott Opera Company, of 60 cast members, who will present the "Bohemian Girl." The new opera house is one of the finest in Central New York and its erection is a source of pride in the people of this vicinity. The scenery has arrived from Rochester and is being rapidly placed in position. On the evening of October 7th, there will be an audience present, large enough in numbers to show that the enterprise of Messrs. Deimel & Schermer is properly appreciated.*

The **Herkimer Democrat, October 15, 1884**, reported, *Deimel & Schermer's New Opera House – On Tuesday evening, of last week, Emma Abbott and her brilliant company opened Deimel & Schermer's Opera House with the "Bohemian Girl."*

About a thousand people witnessed the play (opera). People were present from Mohawk, Ilion, Frankfort, Newport, Little Falls and Utica.

Before the announcement of the opera, Rev. Dr. Powell, pastor of the Universalist Church, made a brief and very interesting address on "The Pulpit, the Press and the Stage." He said that the title of his remarks included three great powers in civilization. While each had its defects and shortcomings, it remained with the people who supported them to say what they should be.

With special reference to the stage – music and the drama – Mr. Powell said that if the good people of Herkimer and vicinity refused to patronize unworthy attractions that might be offered, they would soon be withheld; if they gave generous support to good, worthy and inspirative premonitions and fine music, they would be furnished with what suited their tastes.

After complimenting the enterprise and public spirit of the gentlemen who had erected the beautiful place of amusement, he said he would give way for America's "Queen of Song, Miss Emma Abbott," and her English Opera Company. Mr. Powells remarks were warmly applauded.

Mr. J. J. Flanagan, of The Observer, who was present during the evening, has the following to say of the opera house and its proprietors:

"The people of Herkimer and vicinity owe Messer's. Deimel & Schermer a debt of gratitude for their public spirit and enterprise in erecting for them one of the most beautiful opera houses in the state.

The house is within the third story of the Deimel & Schermer Block, on Main Street, half a block from the Central Depot. It is approached by a broad and easy staircase, on the south side of the block. The auditorium will accommodate 1, 100 persons easily. The floor is graded so that every seat commands a full view of the stage, and each one is favorably located.

In the rear of the parquets are a number of cozy private boxes, with fine outlooks. The presidium boxes are admirably arranged so as to command a full view of the stage and audience, and they are handsomely fitted. The gallery occupies about two-thirds of the rear of the hall and is so gracefully designed as to be no obstruction to light or view. Only the sides reach over the main auditorium, the rear being over the lobby.

The chairs are of the latest design of wood, with neat iron frames and brass figures. The numbers are in consecutive order from south to north. Under each seat is a very convenient wire attachment for a hat holder.

The chairs are roomy and exceedingly comfortable, and the spaces between the rows are all that can be desired.

The ceiling is high, cupola forms in the center. A handsome crystal chandelier is suspended from the center, the heat from the lighted gas assisting in ventilating the hall, through an opening around the pipe.

Gas fixtures are arranged on the outer edge of the gallery and over the boxes. The stage is well lit with side and depressed foot fixtures. A neat brass rail protects the dresses of the performers from the footlight.

The decorations on the walls, ceiling and boxes are of pretty and pleasing designs and harmonious colors. The stage fittings, scenery, etc., are neat, appropriate and convenient. The drop curtain is a well-painted marine harbor scene with an artistic border.

Standpipes, with hoses attached, for fire purposes, are conveniently arranged.

When lighted, the universal compliment was that Herkimer's opera house was a picture, commodious, convenient and elegant in all appointments and fitting from the lobby to the stage.

The **Grand Opera House** was situated on the third floor of the then **Deimel & Schermer Block** on **North Main St.**, in downtown **Herkimer, NY**. Later, this block would be renamed the **Grogan Block**.

The building still stands, as of this writing, as a part of the **Munger Block**, housing the **Wakefield Furniture** store.

According to "**History of the Grand Opera House in Herkimer 1884 – 1917**," written by **Susan Perkins**, retired **Director** of the **Herkimer Historical Society**, "*The third-floor construction began in 1883 for the Grand Opera House, but not quite completed according to the Sanborn Insurance Map of July 1884.*

Susan continues in part, *The first floor of Deimel & Schermer was their dry goods store. On the second floor were a millinery shop, café, a tailor shop, and New York State offices. In the rear were dressing rooms for the performers at the opera house.*

To get to the Grand Opera House, you had to walk a flight of stairs to the second floor on either side of the Deimer & Schermer department store. The stairs ascended to the right of the box offices for the opera house. The box office was located on the second floor.

Tickets cost fifty cents to three dollars, depending on where you were seated. There were two rows of seats with three aisles and a seating capacity of about 1,200. Presidium (executive) boxes were on each side of the walls and were the best seats in the house.

There was a balcony which was located along the rear wall which faced North Main Street. It seated 300 people. The stage was on the North Washington Street side of the building. There was at one time an eight-tiered 100 light chandelier hanging from the middle of the ceiling. The walls were decorated with tan embossed paper with contrasting wine-colored borders. The drapes had been used as curtains for the stage. They were replaced by a drop curtain with advertisements from local merchants printed on the front.

The Deimel & Schermer Grand Opera House building was sold at auction on December 30, 1898, to Louis Schermer for $90,000.

Benjamin Schermer (1872-1955), son of Louis and Sarah (Kraus) Schermer (1845-1929), was the bookkeeper in the clothing store until 1898. He then managed the opera house from 1895 – 1915.

William A. Douque (1816 – 1870), the son-in-law who married their daughter Ruby (1873 – 1961) bought moving pictures to Herkimer. He started out in the Fick Building which was located on South Main Street near the trolley station, but soon needed a bigger place. Douque moved the theater over to the Grand Opera House and then became the manager of the Grand Theater. He Sold the theater and became the State traveling representative of several of the large motion picture film producing companies.

Thomas Grogan (1860 – 1918) bought the Grand Opera House Block in 1916 using the ground floor for his clothing store.

On October 2, 1917, he began the dismantling of the Grand Theater (opera house) making way for a dancing academy and amusement hall. The stage and seats were removed and a new floor was installed. It was expected to be completed in six weeks.

.   The final years of the **Grand Opera House** can be summed up in three newspaper articles from the files of the **Herkimer County Historical Society** listed below. Although each article is **dated,** none has a **source** noted on them.

April 15, 1915: Purchases Grand Opera House Block, Thomas Grogan, a Prominent Merchant of the Village Becomes Owner of Fine Business Block – Will Later Remodel the Building and Occupy it – Worked for Deimel and Schermer in Block. He Now Owns Twenty Years Ago.

Herkimer, N. Y. April 15th *– Thomas M. Grogan one of Herkimer's most prominent and progressive businessmen closed a deal yesterday whereby he acquired the Grand Opera House block property situated on North Main Street. The block is one of Herkimer's most imposing structures and was erected some 20 or more years ago, and at the time was one of the largest blocks in the village. It is now occupied by S. H. Miller Store, the John Campbell furniture store and undertaker parlors and the E. B. Fairchild shoe store on the first floor.*

The second floor is partly occupied by Mr. Campbell and the balance is devoted to the millinery establishment of Miss Cummings and offices.

The third floor is the location of the Grand Theater. The present occupants of the building have leased which have two years to run, after the expiration of which Mr. Grogan will remodel the building and will occupy the ground floor for his clothing business which is rapidly outgrowing its present location.

Mr. Grogan is one of Herkimer's self-made men and his many friends join in congratulating upon his business success.

About 20 years ago he worked as a clothing salesman for Deimel and Schermer in the same block that he purchased yesterday. Resigning his position he decided to seek employment in the city of Buffalo, and while waiting for a west bound train, an acquaintance suggested to him that he better remain at home and embark in business. He borrowed a small amount of capital and started business in one of the smaller stores on Main Street. About 12 years ago he leased the location that he now occupies and since that time has purchased the block where he now is doing business, having remodeled his store, becoming one of the largest clothing stores between Ithica and Schenectady.

December 21, 1915: Little Falls Man Leases Grand Opera House *– The Grand Opera House goes under new management January 1ˢᵗ. The theater has been leased by James A. VanAlstine of Little Falls and the place will open under the new management with two weeks of repertoire plays by a capable company.*

The Grand Opera House, one of the older of Herkimer's modern business blocks, will see many changes in the coming year in its tenants, all of whom have occupied the building for many years. The building is to be occupied on the ground floor by its present owner, Mr. Grogan, with his large clothing business. Tenants who will vacate are the S. H. Miller store which will have quarters in the new Nelson corner of Main and Albany Streets. The E. B. Fairchild shoe store will have quarters in the same building. Campbell's furniture store will remove to a new block its owner is erecting on the former Deimel property on East Albany Street.

December 2, 1917: Herkimer Without A Playhouse – Dismantling of the Grand Underway – To Be Transformed into a Fine Dancing Academy and Amusement Hall – Was Built by Deimel and Schermer in 1883.

Herkimer is without a theater except for the moving picture house which has become so popular as to make the playhouse proposition anything but a financial success. This is not only so in Herkimer but the same condition exists in the larger towns and cities everywhere. This morning the dismantling of the Grand Theater which was constructed in 1883 by Deimel & Schermer was under way.

T. M. Grogan, the owner, intends making the theater into a fine dancing academy and amusement hall, which when finished will be second to none in the Empire State. The stage and seats are to be removed and a new floor placed in the hall which will be about 120X53.

Dressing and smoking rooms are to be provided and the hall is bound to be a popular one on account of the many advantages it will offer. It is expected that the work will be completed in about six weeks in time for the dancing season.

Today, the old **Grand Opera House** lies in ruins waiting to once again be returned, through a state grant, to its previous glory.

Emma Abbott
(1850-1891)
American Operatic Soprano and Impresario
Stared in the Grand Opera House's
Opening Night Production
"Bohemian Girl"
October 7, 1884

The Diemel & Schermer
Grand Opera House
North Main St., Herkimer, NY
1906
Resized from original.

=EPILOGUE=

Of all the varying memories which past **Munger's** employees and shoppers alike had concerning **Munger's Department Store**, one such memory stands out as being common among many, I have uncovered.

The Memory of the Christmas Season at Munger's!

Past employee Tim Adams shares the following: "The store itself was never seen decked out in its Christmas splendor, with decorations inside and out, until the grand unveiling the day after Thanksgiving of each year.

"During the evening and on into the morning hours, following Thanksgiving day, a special team of decorators, from NYC, came to Herkimer to give the store a Christmas 'once over.'

"All the front window displays were then covered with brown paper to prevent anyone from peaking before the unveiling the next morning. Then the team would work its magic.

"The following day, the paper came down from the outside display windows as the store opened to the holiday excitement of one and all as Christmas had indeed arrived at the old Munger's store."

———————————

A note, from an anonymous source, tells the following story of a **1957 Christmas buying trip** to **Munger's:** My Mom had gone Christmas shopping one evening in Herkimer, a neighboring village of ours, and came home so excited over what she had seen in H. G. Munger's Department Store. This store was special. You would always do your holiday shopping there.

"From the time you opened its doors – you were put in the Christmas spirit. Christmas music was playing and every part of the store was decorated and beckoned you in to see the sights and hear the sounds of Christmas. The main floor had jewelry, purses, scarves, hats, gloves and perfumes on one side and Men's apparel on the other. The back of the store had cards, loose candy and roasted nuts in big glass cases, gifts of all types – cookies, cheeses and fancy paper products. This part of the store had a wonderful cozy feeling.

"In the middle of the main floor was the most magnificent staircase leading downstairs. It was all open-air and had a circular wrought iron balcony overlooking the stairs. The staircase split at the bottom to go left or right.

Continued on the next page.

"To the left was beautiful China, silver, crystal and lamps, and to the right was Santo and the North Pole. There were ornaments, decorations and gifts. There was an elevator and a man who operated it. Upstairs from the main floor was Women's apparel. It was filled with overstuffed chairs & 'floor to ceiling' mirrors. You went to the dressing rooms to try on clothes and then you paraded in front of the mirrors and anyone seated in one of those chairs saw the fashion show.

"Also on this floor was the ladies' room. There was also a small private balcony overlooking the main floor that had high white wicker chairs and 'floor standing' ash trays. I always enjoyed sitting there and watching everything going on. When I was 19, having a cigarette there was very fashionable."

———————

Yes, the memories of Christmas at Munger's, from long ago, remain forever clear in the minds of multitudes of those who once shopped there!

"The Christmas-ladened display windows, brightly adorned, and the festive interior of the store, which presented a holiday charm all of its own, were their favorite Munger's memories," I was told.

———————

Over the course of writing this book, I have spent countless hours researching at the **Frank J. Basloe Library** in downtown **Herkimer, NY.**

One afternoon my wife, who had come to the library to pick me up after a day of research, struck up a conversation with a woman she encountered in the library. She told the woman that I was writing a book about the history of the **Munger's** Department Store.

With this, the woman's eyes lit up as she exclaimed, "**You know, Munger's had the 'real' Santa Claus!**" She continued. "He was on the bottom floor of the store and was dressed in pure red velvet!!"

Relaying this experience to my wife, the woman saw herself once again, as a child, mystified upon seeing this magical, shiny, robust figure.

"**Truly**," she said, "**Munger's did have the 'Real" Santa Claus!**"

Thomas Lee Johnson
Author

ABOUT THE AUTHOR

Thomas Lee Johnson was born in Marion, Ohio, in 1949, and grew up in several different towns and small communities in that state, finally moving, with his family, to Chillicothe, Ohio, where seven years later he would graduate from Chillicothe High School.

After graduation, Tom enlisted in the U.S. Navy during the Vietnam War, where he served aboard the guided missile destroyer U.S.\$. Mitscher, DDG-35, obtaining the rank of third-class Boatswain's Mate.

Following his discharge, Tom entered the Columbus State Community College in Columbus, OH where he graduated with an associate degree in Retail Mid-Management. Over the years which followed, Tom worked for several large retail chains in several different states: Ohio, Delaware, Virginia and then ending up in New York State.

It was here, in Herkimer, NY, that Tom would meet and marry Mary Falcone. They would have two daughters: Amanda and Stephanie.

During the early 1990's, Tom spent five years away from retailing, working as an on-air announcer for WJIV Christian Radio in Cherry Valley, NY.

Among Tom's many hobbies are genealogy, magic, the Broadway theatre, and whittling. He specializes in handcrafting & carving walking sticks and canes, for which he has won several blue ribbons, over the years, at the local county fair.

As a child, Tom was a member of television's first generation of viewers, becoming an avid watcher of the NBC children's show, the Howdy Doody show. Today, Tom, a collector of Howdy Doody memorabilia, boasts of being the first official member of The Doodyville Historical Society, founded in 1979, an organization devoted to keeping the memory and history of Howdy alive. Tom is currently retired and living with his first wife, of forty years, Mary, in Frankfort, NY., a small town near Herkimer, NY. Here he spends his time relaxing, researching, writing and whittling.

Author Thomas Lee Johnson, seated at the historic Savoy Restaurant's bar, Rome, NY, at the exact spot where author Alex Haley, legal pad and pen in hand, Is said to have worked on his novel "Roots." Alex was a frequent guest of the restaurant. The Savoy Restaurant, 255 E. Dominick St., Rome, NY, was established in 1908 by the Destito family, who operated it continually until July 2022, when it was "permanently closed" and put up for sale. As of this writing, the Savoy is still closed and "for sale."

Tom has also authored:

CLYDE: THE OLD WHITTLER'S BRANT'S FAMILY STORE

"Stop and Whittle Awhile"

Researched & Written by

Thomas Lee Johnson

"THE OLD WHITTLER"
Clyde Brant

CLYDE BRANT
"The Old Whittler"

The history of the
J. H. Brant Co. & General Store
In operation from 1895 – 1943 in
Lucasville, Scioto Co., Ohio

"The Old Whittler"
Clyde Brant, Proprietor & founder of
"The Whittlers' Clubs of America"
National Headquarters
Brant's General Store
Lucasville, Ohio

Published & Sold Exclusively by
Lucasville Area Historical Society
291 West Street
Lucasville, Scioto Co., Oh

Additional Photos

Earl Block Fire 1917

Rebuilding Earl Block after 1917 Fire

Herkimer Centennial Star Theatre

Interior Munger's

MUNGER'S EMPLOYEES